I0150836

# The Moment

## The Secret Joy Hidden
## Beneath the Sorrows of Life

## Austin De La Pena

One Leaf Publishing
Austin, Texas

First Edition – January 2019

One Leaf Publishing

ISBN-13: 978-0-9996383-1-6

As always, for Carolyn

# CONTENTS

## The Book of Questions

## THE MOMENT

# ACKNOWLEDGMENTS

Given that I am, as you are, nothing more or less than the totality of existence, I must now acknowledge everything that exists, including you, rocks and trees, Krishna and Christ, Alan Moore, Woody Allen, David Lynch, Star Trek, Monty Python, The Young Ones, The Beatles, cats and dogs, the Quantum Field, molecules, and the chair I'm sitting on as I write this. And so I offer my thanks to all that, which is only The Moment.

That said, I will fall back to the consensual hallucination of duality long enough to thank my wife Carolyn, without whom this book would not exist. Carolyn, thank you for enduring these many years of moodiness, brooding, and depression...not to mention my many rants over dinner and drinks regarding the true nature of existence and the logical implications of The Moment.

Although I read a vast number of books during my self-imposed exile, I would finally like to acknowledge, with love, respect, and gratitude, the man whom I consider my guru: Alan Watts. Though I was too young to ever meet him in person, his writings put my feet on the path of knowledge that led to my realization of The Moment. His wisdom was a shining constant beacon in my personal darkness, and his words remain an inspiration for me to this day.

# INTRODUCTION

Since the dawn of recorded history, man has been seeking the answer to the ultimate question: why am I here, and where am I going? Life at times appears to be a cruel folly. It seems we are born as solitary creatures, cast into an uncaring universe and given nothing of permanence to cling to, save the certainty that one day we will die. Accordingly, many approaches to dealing with this problem have developed over the centuries, practical coping mechanisms like philosophy, religion, science, and even denial. Everyone seeks some kind of refuge from this fatalistic certainty, even if that refuge is simple distraction, the idea that if we keep busy enough, pursuing work or sensual pleasures, we won't have time to dwell on the grim reality that everything with a beginning must have an ending. Distraction is an effective strategy in the short term, but in the end any approach that doesn't directly address that ultimate question is merely a bandage over a wound that stubbornly refuses to heal. Knowing this, committed seekers of wisdom, facing the problems of mortality and futility squarely, have understood that the only true refuge from life's intractable problems is the complete knowledge of existence known variously as moksha, nirvana, satori, or enlightenment.

In ancient times, seekers of enlightenment across all religious and philosophical traditions would withdraw from the world — to forests, to monasteries, to locked rooms — attempting to investigate the nature of reality without the distractions of the phenomenal world. It is said that one who attains enlightenment realizes existence is not what it appears to be. Upon attaining enlightenment, all the seeming problems of life vanish for such a person, and he or she goes through life with an unshakable inner peace that springs from a knowledge of the absolute rightness of creation.

This process of withdrawing from the world has characterized my own personal quest for enlightenment. For the last twenty years, I have lived a life of isolation and contemplation — not the isolation of the ashram, or the silence of a monk in his lonely cell, but the isolation of depression, the sense of not belonging in this world that keeps you confined in a prison cell, even in the midst of a crowd. Ironically, I was at the height of my success when depression found me. Even as my career creating computer games and comics was blossoming, I suddenly realized that all my creative and commercial success felt hollow. In a flash I understood that no matter what I achieved, it would never be enough to dispel the empty feeling I had inside, the sense that something critical was missing. I saw that I was using my work as a narcotic, an anodyne to a terrible underlying sense of futility, and nothing I achieved or distracted myself with would ever do anything but numb me temporarily. I would always need more.

Depression followed fast on the heels of this realization. Emotionally, as well as physically to the extent it was practical, I withdrew myself from the daily grind of life. Though I continued to move about in the world, to work and interact with people as required, I would take comfort in solitude whenever possible; solitude, and the study of every esoteric text I could lay my hands on.

I was seeking a higher level of perception, a way of looking at life that would make me feel less empty. During these past few decades, I caught glimpses of this higher awareness in books like *The Bhagavad Gita*, the *Tao Te Ching*, the *Dhammapada*, *The Book* by Alan Watts, the Gnostic Gospels, and various works focusing on quantum physics and the science of consciousness. While these invaluable books, along with many others, moved me deeply and inspired me to further inquiry, none of them led me to the kind of enlightenment I was seeking. In desperation, I began not simply seeking answers, but formulating them for myself, questioning what I read and then exploring possible answers to those questions in my journals. After many years of struggle I realized that in attempting to bridge inconsistencies between these various works, seeking a kind of unified vision of the conscious universe that would be coherent and logically consistent, I had created a unique synthesis of these works, a vision that integrated the traditional core idea of the universe as a nondual consciousness with a new approach to the problems of suffering, evil, and self-determination. In short, because there was no one book that succinctly told me, in plain English, everything that I needed to know, I decided to write one.

My goal in writing *The Moment* was not only to clearly articulate my integrated vision of reality, but also to distill my twenty years of inquiry into a book short enough to be read in one sitting. I wanted to convey, in as short a space as possible, everything that can be conveyed in words regarding that indivisible process of manifestation I call The Moment. While The Moment cannot be comprehended solely through words, in my own quest to know The Moment, words were my springboard. I read everything I could about philosophy, religion, quantum physics, psychology, self-help, and mysticism. No matter how much I read, how much I logically understood the concepts, I could not seem to internalize my knowledge of The Moment until, finally, I began writing this book. Once I did, just like that, everything changed.

Suddenly and without warning, in setting down these words, I came to know The Moment. I don't understand exactly how this happened. Some take decades of study and frustration before they come to this knowledge; others receive it suddenly, without looking for it at all. These words that transformed my own life may spontaneously imbue you with that same knowledge of The Moment, or it may take many readings of this book, or a survey of other books before you cease to seek comprehension and gain true knowledge...I can't say. But I know this book has the potential to change your life because it changed mine.

This work is divided into two books, placed out of logical order: *The Book of Answers*, and *The Book of Questions*. The first book is spare and poetic. In the same way the *Tao Te Ching* was composed thousands of years ago, *The Book of Answers* is written tersely, in acknowledgment of the limited ability of language to convey ultimate truths. In very short order, *The Book of Answers* conveys everything you need to know directly, without complicated explanations, and reading it may lead you to awareness of The Moment if you're in the right state to resonate with the message. Mystics across the centuries, in every religious tradition (including no tradition at all) have suddenly and without warning received the truth regarding The Moment, understanding in every fiber of their beings the perfection and unity of creation. It is possible that reading *The Book of Answers* may trigger this life-changing epiphany within you.

*The Book of Questions*, on the other hand, asks the questions that would logically arise in response to the answers of the first book. When I was searching for the hidden truth of The Moment, I needed an intellectual basis for enlightenment before I could actually internalize this knowledge; accordingly, I've written *The Book of Questions* to provide more detailed explanations of the concepts presented in *The Book of Answers* for those who need them, just as I did.

Answers before questions — the two books are presented out of logical order to reflect the negation of logic and chronology that is the heart of The Moment. Thus, in a sense, this book is unending; *The Book of Answers* leads into *The Book of Questions*, which then again loops back to *The Book of Answers*. If you are, as I was, possessed of a logical and analytical nature and you find yourself impatient with or puzzled by *The Book of Answers*, then by all means skip it and turn to *The Book of Questions*. But if you have the patience to linger over the first book before plunging into the second, if you can allow your mind to wander between those lines, you may find answers of your own stirring within you.

Sometimes inspiration and insight can strike suddenly, with only a nudge. Even if this doesn't happen for you, musing over the first book may help prepare the ground of your mind for the ideas to follow, like plowing and fertilizing a field before the planting of seeds. How you approach this work is entirely your choice. Trust your instincts. They'll be right for you.

There are some terms used consistently in this book: The Moment, The Divine and, occasionally, "God". Please note that when I use the word "God" I do so to put the awful baggage of that word to effective use. It is a convenient shorthand for the concept of an omnipresent creative consciousness only so long as the reader doesn't link that word with the idea of a bearded judgmental boss lording it over us from his throne in the sky. That is not what I mean when I speak, reluctantly, of "God". Please bear that in mind at all times.

Additionally, when I use the term "The Divine" to reference the creative consciousness permeating The Moment, you should know that I'm not attributing any kind of special religious significance to that consciousness. There is no particular reverence in my use of the phrase; as you read on you'll understand that The Divine, far from being a grand and wondrous personage, is embodied in the most base and mundane aspects of existence, and if anything, in choosing that name I'm trying to convey the grandeur and wonder found in the most base and mundane aspects of existence! So those of you with an anti-religious or agnostic bent should not be discouraged from reading on by my use of that term. The

Moment has nothing to do with religion, and everything to do with discovering the basis of existence itself, evidence for which can increasingly be found these days on the cutting edge of science.

As you read through the various sections, you'll find the same themes repeated — sometimes in different ways, other times verbatim. This is by design, since repetition is one of the ways we learn. While I'm tempted by Strunk and White to strip this book down to the bone, stating every principle only once and thereby omitting needless words, I feel a certain amount of repetition will help the message sink in. If you find yourself irritated at some point, reading a passage while impatiently thinking "all right already, I get it", that's a sign not of failure, but of success; if by the end of this book you've come to know The Moment that well, then my work is done.

This book is the culmination of my life's work, though I had no idea when I started seeking the truth of The Moment some two decades ago that it would be so. I started down this path solely to ease my own pain — my depression, my sense of alienation, a feeling of utter frustration and desperate futility. I hope that you're in a better place as you read these words than I was when I began my journey...but if you're not, if you're feeling as miserable now as I was then, then I want you to know that things *can* get better. Don't abandon hope...the knowledge contained in these pages turned my life around. It made me realize the almost unbearable beauty lurking beneath the darkest corners of this experience we call life. It took me a large chunk of my life to realize the truths I've condensed into this narrow volume. It is my fervent hope that in reading this you will come to know The Moment, and in knowing it, you will realize and embrace the miracle that you truly are. And even if it takes you a few readings, over a few years, to come to know The Moment, take just this much on faith, direct from someone who knows: The Moment is joy. And you are always invited to experience it.

# The

# Book

# of

# Answers

# I

The beginning was The Divine:
Featureless, timeless,
Without dimension, without limits,
Beyond conception, beyond manifestation;
Nothing could be said of it
Until The Divine desired to speak,
And so there came The Word,
And the Word was Division:

The light from the dark,
The earth from the heavens,
The sea from the land,
And each from the All.

The Word divided The Divine
Conceptually from itself
And The Word was The Moment
And The Moment was good.

II

Each seeming moment is only The Moment.
Every seeming part of it is only the whole.
Its ways are not its own;
Know it therefore by what it is not:

Containing time, it is not bound by change;
Containing thought, it cannot be comprehended;
Containing space, it cannot be confined;
Containing evil, it can suffer no affront;
Containing fear, it has no need of bravery;
Containing death, it can never cease.

The Moment revels in being what it is not;
It can always be found in its contradictions.

# III

One cannot directly say what The Moment is
For it is also what it is not.

Unbounded by the limits of reason
It eludes all logical partitions
In its play of This and That.

In its contradictions, find its consistency;
Intuit its secrets by surveying its flaws:

Lost, know there is nowhere it is not;
Afraid, know there is no fear at its root;
Angry, know rage is its stranger;
Sad, know that peace is its nature;
Seeking, know it is already found;
Dying, know it surely has no end.

Achieving nothing, it is beyond failure;
Wanting nothing, it is beyond desire;
Free of contention, it is beyond good or evil,
Beyond unity, it has no opposites:

High and low cannot measure it,
Black and white cannot color it,
Up and down cannot direct it,

Rise and fall cannot track it,
Here and there cannot enclose it,
Now and then cannot quantify it.

The Moment is always high and low,
It is always black and white,
Rising and falling, up and down,
Here and there, now and then
All at once, and never at all.

In contradiction find the play
Of the eternally consistent;
In limitation observe the way
Of the manifest limitless.

# IV

One taking his leisure
Escapes not to his mean —
The clerk tallies not his columns;
The referee officiates no match;
The judge hears no case;
The butcher chops no meat;
In their leisure they take delight
In doing what they do not do.

So it is with The Divine:
Shapeless, it hides in the myriad forms;
Untroubled, it delights in the vexation of woes;
Fearless, it cowers before illusory terrors;
Incomprehensible, it binds itself with concepts;
Nameless, it ties itself in words;
Joyful, it surrounds itself with miseries;
Timeless, it surrenders itself to death.

Assured of eternal existence
It plays at finding the end of things.

# V

The Moment is never comprehended
Even when it is known:

Words can be spoken of it;
Thoughts can be set against it;
Opinions can be formulated regarding it;
Consistency may be sought within it;
Measure may be taken of it —

But words only reflect it;
Thoughts are bound by it;
Opinions flail within it;
Consistency cannot confine it;
Measure breaks against it.

The Moment is mysterious, yet easily known
Though never by words or thoughts;
Nor through the tyranny of consistency;
Nor captured by any measure.

Opinions
Formed of thoughts and words,
Measuring for consistency,
Are mired in the delusion of The Moment,
The play of This and That;
Delusions wrapped in a delusion —

# THE MOMENT

Puzzle pieces that never interlock
But laid loosely together form their picture.

Ever vague is its image;
Ever sharp are its paths.

# VI

The Moment is not divided
Except through the scalpel of attention,
And the blade of The Word.

Attention separates
Here from There,
Now from Then,
Self from Other,
This from That;
Fragments of attention,
Named by The Word,
No more capture The Moment
Than a bucket pulled from the ocean
Captures a wave.

The Word serves The Moment
But can never speak its truth.
Go through the Nine Billion Names
To find the Nameless;
Discard Past and Future
To inhabit the nameless Now;
Free of the division of labels
You will truly know The Moment.

The use of a bowl lies
In its empty space.

Empty your mind
To find its best use.

# VII

Anything that can be said about The Moment
Is incomplete.
Any thought regarding The Moment
Can only be inadequate.
Silence is its best ambassador,
Though even silence implies sound;
And so its unity
In even the purest of thoughts
Is ever lost.

Cultivate awareness without comment
And the world will be opened within you;
Only then can you comment truthfully,
In perfect awareness
That you are commenting falsely,
Making perfect sense.

# VIII

The Moment can never be held in the mind.
Being mind, it cannot contain itself;
But even so, being The Moment,
Who can fail to know it?

Knowledge is to understanding
As experience is to comprehension.

My heart knows how to beat —
I don't understand how to beat it;
Messages spark along my nerves —
I don't understand how to send them;
My cells reproduce as they will within me —
I don't understand their divisions;
How skillfully my eyes work
Though I haven't the skill to work them!

The heart beats, but without instruction,
The nerves spark, but without direction,
The cells divide, but without supervision,
The eyes focus, but without operation!

The body functions knowledgeably;
No one understands its ways.

# IX

How impenetrable to my comprehension
Are the ways of my own brain!
The way it forms thoughts
In defiance of my will;
Assembling from vibrations the vastness of the
world
Instantly, effortlessly, without reflection;
Moves my arms to arrest my fall
Before I know I've fallen;
Evokes entire worlds in dreams
Even as I slumber —

While I will never understand my brain
There is nothing I know better.

X

Between This and That
Lies the delusion of Division;

Between Lost and Found
Lies the illusion of Separation;

Between the Wave and the Ocean
Lies the trick of Attention;

Between Good and Evil
Lies the fiction of Other;

Between Merit and Blame
Lies ignorance of The Moment;

Between Success and Failure
Lies the conceit of Achievement;

Between Contentment and Discontent
Lies the futility of Clinging;

Between The Divine and The Moment
Lies the constant of Change;

Between the Sage and The Moment
Lies nothing at all.

# XI

Judgment divides The Moment;
The Moment is indivisible;
What judgment then
Must fall on judgment?

Judge a measure too small
And miss the larger portion;

Judge a measure too large
And miss the finest point;

Judge an action unworthy
And merit eludes you;

Judge another a fool
To become the object of scorn;

Gossip about another
To reveal your own secrets;

Judge yourself lacking
To starve at the banquet.

Judgment is the essence of The Moment —
There is nothing more foreign to it.

# XII

The cat does not purr,
The cat is the purring;
The willow dances not,
The willow is the swaying;
The sun does not radiate,
The sun is the shining.

The cat is the purring
Along with the ears that hear;
The willow is the swaying
Along with the breeze that blows;
The sun is the shining
Along with the eyes that see:

Sun and radiance,
Cat and purr,
Willow and breeze
Are lines drawn on a map —
Do not be fooled by such distractions;
They surely lead to bewilderment.

# XIII

One day blue skies,
One day rain;
One does not speak of weathers —
There is only the weather.

The demarcation between
The front of a storm
And its end
Is misunderstanding.

Is not the storm movement
As well as rain?
With its high pressure edge
Goes its low pressure wake;
Absent movement
What is a storm?

So it is with The Moment:
What comes is what goes.

The demarcation between
The edge of this moment
And the next
Is misunderstanding.

One does not speak of moments —
There is only The Moment.

# XIV

Know it through eyes that see
Sight without words;
Know it through ears that hear
Sound without thoughts;
Know it through lungs that breathe
Scents free of comment;
Know it through skin that accepts
Touch without focus.

In conceptual silence,
Absent all labels,
It can at last be known.

# XV

The Infant knows The Moment
Saying nothing
Beyond thought
Delighting in this and that
Crying in accord
With the shifting of the world.

The Man lives and dies in ignorance
Fearing pain, seeking pleasure,
Hunting advantage, plotting achievement,
Judging failure, assigning blame,
Blinded by darkness, blinded by light,
A fraction among the myriad fractions —
He wanders the maze of separate things
Bewildered by This and That.

The Sage knows The Moment
As he knows himself;
When speaking he says nothing
The Moment would not say;
He thinks no thoughts
Foreign to its ways;
He delights in This and That
Without being taken in;

He does not cry with the shifting of the world
Knowing he is the shifting.
The Sage does less and less every day
Until he does nothing at all,
And then nothing is left undone.

# XVI

I myself do nothing at all
Aside from everything;

I myself am nowhere at all
If not everywhere;

I myself commit every sin
Without the slightest blemish;

I myself suffer every affront
Without suffering at all.

Everywhere, nowhere,
Suffering, in delight,
Doing the something
That is nothing,
I myself am
And am not
Myself.

# XVII

I am
Is the only truth
That can be spoken.

I am
Is the beginning and the end
Of Wisdom.

Doing is always Being,
But Being is not bound by Doing.

Doing here
Being everywhere
Being nowhere
I am.

# XVIII

Within the insignificance of evil
Find its sole significance.

Evil is relational —
One injures another
One takes from another
One hates another
How can there be evil
Without another?

Without evil, without fear,
Without hate, without death,
Without the divisions that delude
What would be the point of The Moment?

One who dwells in a hut on the beach
Does not vacation beside the sea.
The surgeon does not seek respite from routine
By performing surgeries,
As a librarian does not escape daily drudgery
By filing books in another town;
Why would The Divine depart from its peace
To a place of peace?

The Divine is perfect:
Timeless, peaceful, unbounded, free —
The Moment is perfect
In its seeming imperfections:
A play is dull without problems,
A book is tedious without challenges,
A movie is boring without a villain,
A life is interminable without death.

Believing you can remove evil from the world
Without destroying the world
Is believing you can defeat your addiction to air
By stubbornly holding your breath.

# XIX

The evil of The Moment
Is not foreign to perfection:
Evil can no more exist without good
Than a shadow can fall absent light;
Good can no more exist without evil
Than a star can shine without night.

No coin with one side,
No shore bereft of water,
No folly without wisdom,
No surprise absent tedium.

Evil is the bitter taste
That makes the good so sweet.
Do not dwell on this or that mouthful;
Both flavors must fade without trace
At the end of Time
When we return to that place
That is nowhere
And remember ourselves to be
No one at all.

The Moment is a silver screen
Upon which good and evil flicker,
Unstained by the dancing projections
Enjoyed by The Divine.

## XX

Bound within a mirror is a world
Defined by a larger world,
Free of its implications.

A vase is dropped, its image shatters;
Can you cut yourself on the pieces
Of its broken reflection?

The Moment is a mirror
Unblemished by what it reflects.
Nothing of The Moment harms The Divine
As The Divine does unto The Divine
As it would do unto Itself.

# XXI

The Moment's perfection
Is like a mirror,
Reflecting good and evil
Blemished by neither.

The Moment's perfection
Is unlike a mirror,
For what can ever reflect
The form of the Formless?

The Moment's perfection
Is like a screen
Containing projections
Of Divine light.

The Moment's perfection
Is unlike a screen,
For what screen contains both
The image and the Eye?

All thoughts in The Moment
Contain their own contradictions;
No expression of truth within it so pure
As to escape the gravity of argument.

The Moment is a mirror wherein
The Divine contemplates its reflection;
The Moment is a screen upon which
The Divine watches its play;
It is precisely none of these things
Since nothing can be precisely said.

To discuss The Moment at all
One must accept contradiction,
As a diver in murky water accepts
Blurred vision searching for treasure.

# XXII

Evil is the killing of trees
To fashion the planks
That form the stage;

Evil is the destructive fire
Illuminating the myriad players
As they perform their parts;

Evil is the problem in the play
Without which there could never be
The joy of the solution.

Without evil, at curtain fall,
There would be no tears,
And likewise no applause.

# XXIII

Fear is the shadow of courage,
Evil is the shadow of good,
Death is the shadow of life,
Delusion is the shadow of knowledge.

Shadows separate things of light
One from another;
Absent shade, the world would seem
A field of luminous glare.

Shadows grant dimension to the formless,
Give shape to the shapeless,
Cloak the monotony of the continuous
Lend mystery to the known.

Reveling in the sunniest day
Thank the shadows that define it,
That save the rapacious light
From engulfing itself.

The Moment is the shadow of The Divine;
You are the shadow of perfection.

# XXIV

Good is the limit of evil;
Evil takes the measure of good.
Good absent evil is monotonous;
Evil apart from good lacks distinction.
Good is elevated rising above evil;
Evil is ever pushing against the good.

Good circles evil
Like a dog chasing its tail,
Barking in angry delight;
The dog chasing his tail
In playful frustration
Is always the perfect good.

# XXV

The failure of the leaves
Is the success of the winter;

The failure of the winter
Is the success of the blossoms;

The failure of the blossoms
Is the success of the grazing beasts;

The failure of the grazing beasts
Is the success of the hungry man;

The failure of the hungry man
Is the success of his heirs;

The failure of the heirs
Is the success of death;

The success of death
Is the success of life;

The success of life
Is the success of The Moment;

The success of The Moment
Is the success of The Divine;

The success of The Divine
Is the failure of the leaves.

# XXVI

Time is not frames in a film —
Time is the theater screen
Upon which images unfold;

Time is not the falling of leaves
Time is the park where leaves fall,
Gathering into stillness;

The clock does not mark Time —
The clock marks change
Moving within Time.

Time is not a series of fractions
But the equation itself,
Never to be solved in Time.

# XXVII

The Moment is perfect, exactly as it is.
Perfectly manifesting, it always fulfills
Its purposeless purpose.

All that is manifested, seen and unseen,
Forms The Moment, without judgment or need.

Beneath The Moment lies The Divine.
The Divine is to The Moment
As a dream to the dreamer.
The Moment is limited to The Divine
But The Divine is not limited to The Moment.

All that exists is perfection.
The Moment is perfect in its flaws.
The Divine is as perfect in its remove
As it is in its manifestation —
The manifestation of The Moment;
The manifestation of you.

# XXVIII

You do not dwell in The Moment
Any more than wind dwells in air.

You inhabit The Moment no more
Than sand inhabits a beach.

You can escape it as easily
As light flees luminescence.

You are as foreign to The Moment
As reverence to a prayer.

# XXIX

A tree is not lost in the wood;
A drop is not lost in the ocean;
A breeze is not lost in the sky;
A man is not lost in the world.

Find the familiar,
Embrace the strange,
Accept the alien,
Recognize yourself.

# XXX

Where can you go that The Moment is not?
What can you do to trespass against it?
What obstacle can you lay down to hinder it?
What aid can you give to support it?

The Moment is nowhere not;
Its design is ever realized;
All paths follow its way;
Praise and blame are answers
To mistaken questions.

# XXXI

Your eyes are a window
Through which The Divine sees itself.

Your touch is the way
Eternity describes itself.

Your flaws are the way
Perfection delights in itself.

Your wandering is the way
God finds himself.

Your purpose is the perfect way
You have of being yourself.

# XXXII

You exist.
The Moment is all that exists.
You are The Moment.

The Moment is The Divine.
The Divine is perfection.
Recognize yourself.

Consciousness is the unified field
From which all matter springs.
Consciousness is the totality of existence
And the unmanifested Divine:
Recognize in its perfection
The perfection that is your own.

You are a viewpoint of God
From which it regards itself.

# XXXIII

Thoughts chase their like;
The stream of consciousness
Winds through erratic banks
Of careening conception:

Hammer chases nail,
Nail chases coffin,
Coffin chases death,
Death chases skull,
Skull chases Yorick,
Yorick chases Hamlet,
Hamlet chases being,
And not being.

Find in synchronicity
The thoughts of The Divine
Manifesting like to like;
Arranging the world
In accord with what occurs.

Be watchful for its patterns,
Like arising with like —
How like causality are its whims!

# XXXIV

When you know The Moment
You finally know yourself;
Knowing yourself
You know everyone;
Knowing everyone
You know The Divine;
Beyond The Divine
No more can be known.

The Divine is the horizon
At the edge of manifestation;
Beyond understanding,
It is ever known.

There was never a time
When it was your stranger;
Forgetting itself in you
Is the glory of The Moment.

In your ignorance, always mark
The perfection of its purpose.

# XXXV

The Moment is the manifestation
Wherein The Divine could pretend
To limit and define itself
In the play of This and That.

It is essential to the play
Of This and That
For The Divine to forget
It is playing.

To escape infinity, it pretends there are limits;
To escape unity, it pretends to be many;
To escape peace, it pretends there is danger;
To escape eternity, it pretends there is death.

In all of creation —
The myriad universes,
Born of quantum flux,
Across all paths taken,
All trajectories cast —
Only you are uniquely you.

There is no other shade of The Divine like you,
No flavor of The Moment exactly like you:
No memories like yours,
No joys like your own,

No delusions precisely as charming,
No flaws exactly as sweet.
Whatever actions you partake in,
Wherever you go, whatever you do,
You are always perfectly yourself,
Always fulfilling your purpose
Simply by being yourself —
The only window God has,
At your time, in your space,
To gaze in wonder at
His perfect Moment.

The

Book

of

Questions

## *What is The Moment?*

What is *not* The Moment?

Imperfectly put, The Moment is the perpetual unfolding of the entirety of existence. It is a verb without a noun, action without subject. It is the manifestation of pure being in the framework of time and space. It is not a sequence of events, but the one perpetual event itself.

The Moment is the play of a nondual consciousness, here called The Divine, that has created the conditions of Time, Space, and Opposites in order to experience its unity as separation. All features of The Moment, while real manifestations in a physical sense, are illusory in conceptual terms. All seemingly separate beings and objects are merely that unitary consciousness masquerading as the many forms of the material universe. There is no separation. There is only one consciousness, pretending to be many.

Duality is a term describing the condition of containing opposites — light/dark, day/night, high/low, good/evil. Though it appears to be dualistic in nature, in reality The Moment is nondual because all apparent opposites and divisions within The Moment are illusory tricks of attention, infinity surveyed from a finite viewpoint.

Despite the fact that it cannot be named or thought about directly, The Moment is not alien to us, and can therefore be known. The Moment can be known only when you set aside the concepts of separateness and opposites.

# *What is The Divine?*
# *What is its nature?*

The Divine is the consciousness that has manifested The Moment. It is all that truly exists. Because it is nondual, a totality unto itself, it has no opposite; at the root level of being there is nothing that is not The Divine. Having no opposite, nothing purely true can be said of it because all language is dualistic; as soon as you label something, you're automatically separating it from something else. Since any statement applied to The Divine conceptually limits it, any such statement must be fundamentally mistaken in some regard.

To say The Divine is good, for example, implies that there is evil outside of The Divine against which it could be compared. Since there is nothing separate from The Divine, it can be said to be neither good nor evil. Also, since good and evil are relational/transactional states, they can't exist in perfect isolation — without another party, who is there to benefit or to harm? Evil must be inflicted on someone else; after all, harming yourself is not evil. Self-destruction may well be harmful, foolish, ignorant...but not evil. By the same token, doing something beneficial for yourself is applied self-interest rather than genuine goodness.

So what else could you say about The Divine? You can't say The Divine is vast, because it doesn't coexist with anything against which it could be compared...vast as opposed to what? The Divine does not exist in time and space; time and space are features of The Moment, created by The Divine that it might have attributes and thereby experience itself. Without space, nothing can exist possessing mass, or dimension of any kind. In the absence of space, there can be no physical attributes whatsoever.

And so, existing outside of space, The Divine is neither vast nor tiny. Existing outside of time, it cannot be said to be ancient. You cannot even accurately call The Divine infinite, because that implies the existence of a finite object other than The Divine that The Divine is not. Even "The Divine" is a poor name for this underlying consciousness, because it implies that its opposite, The Profane, must exist outside The Divine!

I call it "The Divine" as a point of reference, since I must call it something to discuss it at all. I chose that weighty word because the unnameable self itself fills me with a kind of awe, and I wanted a name that conveyed that feeling; regardless of my personal preference in this matter, no label we apply to it can impose any qualities or limits on the thing itself.

So while we can describe The Divine as infinite, eternal, omniscient, omnipotent, and omnipresent, all these descriptions are limited by language, flawed concepts referring to something beyond conception that exists entirely outside our frame of reference. We exist in a manifested universe. The Divine is not bound by manifestation. Words and symbols give us, at best, a feel for The Divine's true nature, but never an exact representation of it. Whatever we say The Moment *is*, it is in some sense *not* because it embodies all seemingly contradictory states simultaneously. We can only roughly describe The Moment in metaphoric terms, loosely caressing its illusory dimensions with syllables and thoughts bound within the very illusion we're attempting to penetrate. The Divine cannot be understood.

That said, The Divine's nature can be *known* because it is *our* nature, the nature of The Moment. When you truly internalize that all you see, hear and know is the play of The Divine, that this universe is not a mistake but a choice, that The Moment is perfectly serving its purpose by allowing The Divine to manifest in space/time and experience itself, then you realize that everything is perfect exactly as it is, and *you are that perfection. Not a part of that perfection, not a piece of The Moment, but The Moment* itself, *and by extension, The Divine.*

Once you truly know this, you know The Moment as you know yourself, and all problems disappear. You realize there is nothing here to win or lose, nothing you must do, nowhere you must be. You cannot get lost, cannot fail, cannot do other than be what you are — the perfect manifestation of The Divine.

Now when I say that all problems disappear, I mean that in a metaphysical sense: the ultimate problems of personal identity, morality, our purpose in the world, good versus evil, the meaning of life, and the nature of "God". Daily challenges will of course still arise — you will have bills to pay, romantic problems, illnesses and, eventually, death. There are also global problems that will survive our realization of The Moment, problems like world hunger, war, child abuse, animal cruelty, environmental destruction, disease, and personal suffering...we'll address the problem of suffering later in this book, but for now the important thing to realize is when you know your true nature, the dire significance of life's challenges is stripped away. Evil is not what it initially appears to be, the menace of this vast uncaring universe is revealed as something else entirely, and death is robbed of its grave implications when you truly know yourself not as an isolated consciousness trapped in a lonely sack of flesh, but the entirety of the universe, the untroubled source of consciousness, at home everywhere you go.

All of this may, at this point, seem wildly counter-intuitive to you. That's by design. If the universe were easily deciphered, that would defeat its purpose. As for the nature of that purpose, read on...

*Are you saying that I'm a part of The Moment, along with everyone else? That, in a sense, I am everyone else?*

That's not entirely correct. You yourself are not a *part* of The Moment, for The Moment is indivisible...*you* are *The Moment.* Along with everyone and everything else.

We'll spend the rest of this book exploring this truth. It has many ramifications that will completely alter your perception of yourself and the universe. This idea you have of yourself, that you're a separate being in a universe of separate things, is an illusion; similarly, the idea that "you" are the source of your actions is illusory as well. You do not initiate actions independently; all actions are only one action — the grand process of The Moment.

All events, though they appear to be from myriad sources, are only the unfolding of The Moment. Consider the ocean...even though one part of it may be covered in foam while another part is not, in all its parts it is still the ocean, behaving according to its nature, which is to simultaneously manifest diverse states. It is only because we can't see the entire ocean at once that we might say "no, the ocean isn't foamy, it's smooth and blue"; in actuality it is always both at once. It is blue and green, shallow and deep, wavy and calm, all at once without contradiction. It is only our inability to see the ocean in its entirety that seemingly makes these statements contradictory.

So it is with The Moment. All the divisions we cling to from our limited perspectives — high/low, dark/light, good/evil — are simultaneously manifested by and indivisible from The Moment. All divisions are illusory distinctions produced by our myopically finite views of infinity.

The same thing can be said for the division that is you. You are a seemingly separate expression of The Moment that is in reality The Moment itself. Whether you are a sad expression, a guilty expression, or a joyous expression, you are serving as a set of eyes, a pair of ears, a nexus of touch and sound and feeling, through which the consciousness manifesting the universe experiences itself. And therein lies your unalterable perfection.

There are, in all of Creation, no eyes that see the Universe exactly like yours. You are a unique and irreplaceable viewpoint of "God", therefore you serve your purpose perfectly, no matter how you feel about yourself — whether self-loathing or self-loving, angry or forgiving, peaceful or fearful, you are perfectly you and as perfect a part of The Moment as anything that exists.

It doesn't matter to the consciousness that is The Moment how you feel about yourself, or what, if anything, you think of The Moment, because that consciousness, investing itself in this reality, knows existence is simply a joyous play.

So why not join the play?

Why not realize you are The Moment?

Why not abandon guilt and loneliness, and embrace the truth that nothing is separate from you, that the things you seemingly do are only the action of The Moment, and everything that occurs is in accord with its unfolding?

*Why do you believe that everything is one thing
when clearly there's a difference between me and,
say, my kitchen table for example?*

Because you and the table mutually arise. This is
always the case — try as you may to identify two
discrete elements that exist as separate objects, you'll
find there nevertheless exists a connection between
them. For example, superficially, if you were never
born you wouldn't have bought the table. That's a
shallow link, but let's expand it. If the human race
did not exist, there would be no market for tables, nor
would there be anyone to make tables. So tables
necessarily go with humans. But even more to the
point, we humans need tables, and chairs for that
matter, because we're shaped the way we are; because
our knees bend the way they do, because our hands
are higher than our legs, it's useful for us to have a
table to put things on while we're sitting.

Our human form has been shaped by our
environment. Since we exist on solid ground instead
of floating in liquid, we need tables; if we existed in
water, tables would be useless to us. We might use
some kind of stable platforms that float on the
surface if we were still air-breathing mammals, like
porpoises, or we might use stabilized floating
anchored surfaces in the depths if we had gills, but
these structures would not be tables, for tables are

constructed to resist gravity, elevating a stable surface above the ground.

So again…to have tables, elevated planes with legs, you must necessarily have gravity. The shape and density of any table is dictated by the relative strength of that gravity. If the gravity on Earth were higher, of crushing strength like that of Jupiter, the table would be a much different thing. It would be massive, made of some incredibly dense material to withstand the crushing pull of gravity. And, needless to say, without an atmosphere on the planet, there would be no tables because there would be no life to construct them. As far as that goes, then, to have a table you must also have, in addition to gravity and an atmosphere, a sun to warm the planet to support the organisms that make and use the table. Likewise, even though tables are used on land, you must have water to have tables, again to support the life that makes and uses the tables.

Furthermore, to exist at all you must have particles, and you can't have particles without the quantum fields that extrude them. But why stop there? Without the Big Bang, we wouldn't have fields, or particles, land, water, tables…or you, for that matter.

So what exactly is the division between you and the table? Are you two separate objects simply because you differ from the table in behavior and appearance?

Consider a lizard, crawling on a rock. We know it's a lizard because we perceive it in its totality. It's small enough for us to see its entire body at a glance, and we recognize it as a lizard from our previous experience with reptiles. But that said, we can easily shift our attention away from the larger lizard to examine its different parts. We can look at the lizard's eyes, for example. They're definitely different than, say, the lizard's tongue, and the tongue is different from the legs, and the toes are clearly distinguishable from the larger feet. Yet even though we can focus our attention on different parts of the lizard, no matter what part we're singling out for attention, we're still looking at a lizard. The details we selectively notice are not segregated by nature, but only by our concepts, our language, and the process of our attention. For attention is both attending to details, and attenuating other details.

When we pay attention to something, we are selectively focusing on that something and, in the process, inevitably excluding everything else from our consideration in that instant. For example, you can't read two things at once. If you printed two different offset texts on a single page, one text in black and the other printed between the lines of black text in red, you would only be able to read one set of text at a time. Regardless of which text you read, wouldn't both texts remain printed on the page? If you divide a lizard into its component features conceptually, does that impact the lizard's reality as a lizard?

All seemingly separate objects and events in The Moment arise indivisibly together. We can't perceive this normally because we're engineered to notice foreground differences rather than background similarities, but just the same, in the indivisible nondual Moment, there are no separate events. "Events" are subjective divisions, the limited observations of beings too small to perceive the whole process that is The Moment. Events are artificial divisions of an indivisible whole that exist solely as conceptual conceits, rather like lines dividing territory into counties on a map. When cartographers map out their various boundaries, they aren't actually partitioning the land, cutting through the grass and rock and laying down giant lines on the ground. The boundaries they impose are simply mental constructs, convenient concepts for organizational purposes. Again, we understand this easily because we have the perspective to see the entirety of a map; we can draw the lines, and write the names of each county down in the margins. We can also subsequently visit those spots and see there are no lines painted on the grass. These concepts are easy to grasp and come as no surprise. But how much more difficult is it to understand that the divisions imposed by our attention on the universe are equally arbitrary and meaningless?

Let's expand our lizard metaphor: if we were microscopic single cell organisms dwelling on one of the lizard's scales, we would perceive our universe as a green scale (if that...even the scale would probably be too large for us to fathom as anything but "The Surface Upon Which We Ooze"). For the purpose of our little analogy, let's pretend we're still capable of thought despite our microscopic gelatinous state. Regardless of our theories regarding the nature of our Green Scale Universe, perception of the larger lizard would completely elude us. Even if we had some kind of vague inkling that something unseen, too large to glimpse, was going on around us, we would only be able to theorize about the nature of the larger lizard. We would certainly have no ideas regarding the complex processes of the lizard, like its respiratory, digestive or reproductive processes (especially not the reproductive processes, since we reproduce asexually through cellular division). We wouldn't know the lizard eats flies (What are flies?), that it moves around (Around? Beyond our Green Scale Universe?), that it sticks to surfaces (What surfaces? There is only THE green surface, right?), that it needs water and air and arises with people and tables, atmospheres and suns, galaxies and The Big Bang, and any egghead amoeba that suggested there might be more to the universe than The Green Scale would be considered a fantasist. But that wouldn't impact the truth of the matter in the slightest.

So in response to this question — what makes you say all things are one thing — I would challenge you: try to think of something that exists in total isolation from the rest of the universe.

You won't be able to do it. It's impossible. "Empty space", for example, is nothing of the kind. The latest experiments demonstrate that even in the utter emptiness of the vacuum, there is a restless oscillation of virtual particles called zero point motion (also known as quantum fluctuation). Even empty space is filled with continuous fields connecting the entirety of the spacetime continuum. We'll discuss this in greater detail later in the section on scientific proof of The Moment, but suffice it to say for now that nothing exists in isolation. This is a theme we'll return to and reiterate repeatedly because it's at the very core of understanding The Moment. Divisions do not exist. Time is not separate from space, particles do not exist as separate particles but are rather extrusions from continuous universal fields, and not even empty space can be partitioned. All divisions in our universe are illusory mental constructs of attention...and that's why you're not really separate from your table.

*You say there is only The Moment, but what about the passage of time? How can you say there's only one continuous moment when clearly clocks run, people grow old, and seasons change?*

Time does not exist independently of The Moment. Time has no meaning outside the context of manifestation; indeed, it is only time, along with its corollary space, that allows The Moment to exist at all, for it is only in time and space that change and motion can occur. We perceive change and motion as the action of time itself, a perfectly understandable confusion given that we associate the motion of clocks with time passing, internalizing the artificial divisions of hours and seconds as actual divisions of time...but time is not divisible by nature. We mark the divisions of the clock as a shared convention, a convenience that allows us to coordinate with others and mark the seeming passage of our days. Our error lies in confusing our convenient conventions with natural laws. Time is not a series of moments, relentlessly ticking away. There never was another moment, there never will be another. There is no past, no future. There is only The Moment.

We think of time as a series of events occurring serially, in causal chains — this happens, causing that to happen, causing something else to happen and so on — but this is only an illusion of perception, based on a misunderstanding of how The Moment unfolds.

To understand that time is not a phenomenon progressing in minute increments, we should first consider how any divisions of space are equally artificial (space is, for whatever reason, easier to understand than time, even though for all intents and purposes they're pretty much the same thing). Divisions in space are purely observational. We can divide space up into regions — solar systems, galaxies, constellations — but divisions such as these are conceptual, not actual. When we divide space into cataloged sections, space is not actually carved up any more than lines on a map actually slice the physical earth into chunks.

So it is with space's twin, time. We tend to conceptually partition chunks of time in accordance with the occurrence of events — this event happened at this time, that event at that time — but this is a delusion attributable to the subjective nature of our observations. We only perceive the smallest changes in The Moment because our perspective is so very limited. For example, we see weather locally, easily forgetting that the weather is one global system without demarcations. A storm, while seemingly a distinct event separate from the clear skies that preceded it, is actually one system in which the sunny skies elsewhere on the globe played a role in the formation of that regional storm, and neither state could exist independently. In this regard, the seemingly discrete event we refer to as a storm is analogous to a wave on the ocean. No wave is ever separate from the ocean; any division of a wave from the ocean is solely created in the mind of the observer through the process of attention, singling out one feature while ignoring the rest of the larger event. We attend to the wave, and attenuate all the other waves, the surrounding ocean manifesting the waves, and the sky itself — a key element of the wave after all, since the wave wouldn't exist without the air above it to surge into!

In a similar way, our attention divides time into events, and we link these artificially-divided events into chains of causality — this event causing that event, that event causing another one, and so on. You turn on the stove, the water boils; you fall on the sidewalk, you skin your knee. Causality is a common sense assumption based on observation, but our observations are flawed. *Change* occurs in The Moment (it would be static otherwise), but the notion that discrete *events* trigger *other* events is an illusion of limited perception.

To explain the illusion of causality, I'll resort to an analogy: let's pretend that you've spent your entire life confined in a single room alone, isolated in a house on a cliff overlooking the sea (though naturally you don't know it as the sea, since you've never been outside). All you know of the world outside your room is the view from one narrow window on the opposite wall, a pane of glass about a foot wide and ten feet high — your only slice of the world. You are bedridden, and cannot get close enough to the window to change your angle of view — all you ever see is the same narrow slice of reality. You have no background information to apply any context to what you see outside your window, which is mostly static and peaceful.

So looking out this narrow window at the sea, you periodically notice a very strange thing...sometimes a large battleship passes by. You don't know what it is exactly, but you do observe that whenever it appears it always does so in a particular sequence: first you see a pointy part, arrayed with long tubes you can't recognize as gigantic guns...then you see a tower with a spinning dish on the top...then you notice a flat end with flags on it, fluttering in the air. Not understanding the totality of what you're seeing, you come to a conclusion: because the sequence is always the same — guns, tower, flags — you assume that the guns cause the tower, and the tower in turn causes the flags! Because you can't grasp the totality of what the ship is, never having seen the entire ship at one time, seeing only pieces of it through your window, and having no idea it's actually a continuous indivisible object, you assume causality is occurring...one piece causing another piece, causing another piece.

This narrow window is a metaphor for how our consciousness operates, focusing our attention on narrow parts of our surroundings. When we attend to something, when we narrowly direct our attention to one thing, we are concentrating on that one thing to the exclusion of everything else around us. So attention, while seemingly the act of sharpening perception, is actually an exclusionary process, a mental activity dividing and isolating one detail of the indivisible Moment from its larger self. In attempting to deeply enhance our perception, we actually dull our awareness, banishing the entirety of creation (minus one object of focus) to the background of our consciousness!

Attention, the attenuating of boundless reality down to a particular point of interest, is an essential survival skill, facilitating the gathering of food and the avoidance of predators, but we fall into delusion when we believe the details we conceptually divide from the unity of The Moment are in fact separate objects existing independently in reality. The details we attend to are no more divided by our attention than land is divided by lines on a map, or a brain is carved up by the dotted lines in a medical textbook.

So returning to our metaphor of the ship viewed through the narrow window, even knowing what we know (that the ship is a single object, not a front causing a middle causing an end), we still assume that its movement across the water is the result of the passage of time. That is a mistaken assumption. The ship's movement across the water is only change and motion. Time is the bubble that allows the process of The Moment to unfold, for change and motion can only occur in time, but while time creates the space for this unfolding to occur, time is not the unfolding itself.

There is not one moment, then another, then another, like frames in a film. Existence is not like a movie, a staccato flicker of divided instants strung together sequentially to advance a story; the past does not exist in a previous frame that you could jump to, nor is the future contained in frames farther up the reel — rather, time is like a movie screen, a space wherein the movie (The Moment) may play out, and The Divine is like the light that animates The Moment, unfolding on the screen of time. (This analogy is both apt and seriously flawed to the extent that the screen, the light, and the movie are all The Moment, and The Divine would be the screen, the light, the movie, the projector, the theater, and the larger universe...but restrained as we are by our conceptual and linguistic limits, the best we can ever do when discussing The Moment is address it in terms of myth and metaphor. We can only draw imprecise analogies to get a *sense* of what it is *like*, never stating exactly what it *is*...but we'll discuss this at greater length later.)

All divisions are conceptual in nature; so it is with time and space. Physicists will tell you that time and space are inextricably entangled. Indeed, for all practical purposes time and space are indivisible, hence the common use of the term "spacetime". It is space and time that allow The Moment to manifest. Space facilitates movement, and time facilitates change. Space and time correlate inversely: the faster an object moves in space, the slower the object changes in time. This phenomenon is known as relativity, further examination of which would be quite beyond the scope of this book. Suffice it to say that time is not a series of discrete moments running through the projector of life. There are no moments, there is only one Moment, one perpetual bubble of time in which motion and change can occur.

It may seem difficult to think of The Moment as a single event rather than a string of events. After all, it does seem like a wave moves and then dies, that a ball falls, bounces, and rises again, that once I was a child and now I'm grown. To properly grasp its true nature, think of The Moment in this way:

If we were able to suspend the bubble that is Time, freezing all change and motion, then the state of existence frozen in that suspension would be the single event that is The Moment.

Across the face of the Earth, across all the galaxies, in every infinite parallel universe, that would be a snapshot of the manifested consciousness that is "I". Reinstate time for a duration, and then freeze it again...you do not have another "moment", but only the same Moment in a different state. The wave that has changed shape and position, the "you" that has aged, the Earth that has rotated, the galaxies that have hurtled through space, the countless parallel universes existing in contradictory relativistic states — this universe of change and motion is still, when frozen, a snapshot of The Moment.

Thinking of the process of The Moment in terms of a frozen photo makes it easier to understand the vastness of The Moment as a symbolically comprehensible object. Similarly, no matter what TV shows you're watching or what video games you're playing, in the end all those universes are contained in a box in your living room, constrained by the dimensions of one static screen; when you freeze frame the picture, the illusion of independent life is suspended, and you realize all these innumerable cinematic universes you lose yourself in, across all the hundreds of channels, are just one TV set after all.

*Then you're saying that time both does and* doesn't *exist?*

Time doesn't exist outside of manifestation. The Divine does not natively exist in time or space; these qualities were created to enable The Divine to manifest itself as The Moment. Time does exist around/within The Moment, since The Moment could not exist without time. Change and motion are necessary for manifestation to occur, and change/motion can only ever occur within the condition known as time.

Without time, there is nothing but stillness, the static peace native to The Divine one might loosely call Eternity. But time is not a string of moments, one following the other — time is one moment, like an envelope within which the contents can experience change and motion.

*What is the difference between comprehending
The Moment and knowing it? Why can I know
The Moment but never comprehend it?*

Comprehension is a mental process, the intellectual act of understanding. The Moment cannot be understood because you *are* The Moment — not a *piece* of it since there are no divisions, but its *entirety*; accordingly, there's no way you can get outside The Moment to perceive it, in all its complexity, from a superior viewpoint...just as you cannot step outside yourself to see yourself from a distance.

In the same way that you can't understand The Moment from a superior external viewpoint, you can never arrive at an understanding of The Moment solely through the application of thought. Though thoughts are of The Moment, no thought can encompass it. Thoughts are expressed linguistically; even mathematical equations are a form of language, highly abstracted representations of reality that convey information symbolically. Language is comprised of words and symbols representing observed fragments of The Moment conceptually divided from its unity through attention. Language is a poor way to represent The Moment because language expresses reality in linear compartmentalized fragments, and The Moment cannot be fragmented. The Moment, from instant to seeming instant, is nothing less than the entirety of existence. When you look at, or define, anything finite in The Moment, it is no longer The Moment, but only a thought, a symbol, representing The Moment in your mind, a minute focus of attention which is, in turn, nothing more than an exclusion of the vast majority of The Moment, which remains unobserved and too vast to be expressed or comprehended.

Our language, particularly our grammar, is inherently mired in dualism — the notion that the observer/speaker is separate from the rest of the world. Even a simple sentence like "I see a tree" is riddled with errors in terms of the reality of The Moment. To begin with, it inherently assumes a separation between "I" and the tree simply by distinguishing the two nouns! In reality, there is no division between I, the tree, the hill it sits on, the sky, the sun, and the larger universe…seeing these things as separate is only a trick of selective attention. Furthermore, the idea that "I" "see" is the division between noun and verb, an innate convention of our language that reinforces the mistaken idea of separation between the actor and the action. Hopefully at this point you at least conceptually grasp there is only one process unfolding in the universe, and that the actor *is* the action. Therefore, the sentence "I see a tree", while having a certain practical utility in everyday life, is just so fundamentally flawed as to be virtually useless for discussing higher truths.

This sentence is describing the process of seeing, a process that involves both the tree and the observer: without either participating in this process, there is no seeing to be done. Sentences like "I see a tree" are useful enough symbolically for navigating The Moment. If you're hunting squirrels or looking for shade, then "I see a tree" is a serviceable shorthand for communicating some practical information, but it's important to remember that the very structure of language automatically reinforces a bias toward duality in opposition to nondual reality.

Aside from being hindered by structural deficiencies, language is inadequate for describing The Moment due to its symbolic nature. The word "cat" is not an actual cat, and the word "love" is always, at best, a crude approximation of that emotion in all its many complex shades. Words are useful for navigating the phenomenal world, just as money is a useful shorthand for actual wealth. We wouldn't be able to set up a meeting with a friend to see a movie without being able to say "Meet me at 8:10 at the Americana to see *Kong: Skull Island*". "Americana" is shorthand for the theater on North Loop Boulevard, *"Kong: Skull Island"* is shorthand for an event, and "meet me at 8:10" is an agreed-upon convention for the time/space intersection of two apparently separate entities. Those names are symbolic representations of actual locations and events used for convenience, in the same way that money, essentially worthless by itself, symbolically represents real wealth. You can't eat, drink, or enjoy money, but symbolic money can be exchanged for actual things like steaks, martinis, trips to Paris, and reproductions of famous movie robots. Too often we mistake symbol for reality in conceptual terms. We hoard money and think ourselves rich instead of converting money to the richness of actual experience, and we use language not merely as a convenient tool representing reality, but as slices of reality itself.

In short, words represent separate things in a world where separation does not exist. When we too closely identify words with the things they represent, we tend to think of those things as separate.

The Moment is beyond comprehension or expression through word or thought. It is the manifestation of the Infinite in time. Yet while you can never understand The Moment, you *can* come to *know* it...not through thought alone, but through constant awareness of its unitary unfolding.

## *How will I come to know The Moment then, if not through language?*

The best way to know The Moment is through direct experience. When you quiet your mind and receive the unfolding of The Moment without the constant commentary of linguistic thought, you open yourself to feeling it unfolding around you.

You may know The Moment when you cease to identify yourself solely with your body, your thoughts, and your memories. You may come to know it when you expand your self-concept to the larger reality around you, for that in truth is the extent of your manifestation. When you can look at crows in a field and both marvel at them and feel them as extensions of yourself, manifesting in a field of your own, beneath a sky that is you, it will change everything for you.

Your life will no longer be a problem to be solved, a game to win. When you cease to think of yourself as an isolated island of lonely consciousness confronting a universe of separate, possibly hostile things, when you realize your indivisible unity with The Moment, all the seeming problems of life are transformed. While you still experience pain and suffering, for these are inextricably woven into the experience that is manifestation for reasons we'll address soon, the most fundamental concerns of human life — alienation, fear, evil, death — are stripped of their special significance. We still experience these things, but they no longer have such dire and ultimate implications. We see through them to the larger truth of our existence as a vast, wondrous process that will never end, the joyous manifestation of infinite consciousness. We know that we can never be lost, never be abandoned. We never truly lose anyone or anything, including ourselves. There is nothing to be won or lost because life is not a game but a dance to be enjoyed solely for what it is. Life ceases to be a lonely struggle and becomes what it was meant to be — an experience to be lived without any goal other than living.

We'll discuss some techniques for stilling the mind in a later section, but right now I'd like to address this question in a different way. Confirmation that you're on the right track to knowing The Moment will come when you listen openly to the world, and begin experiencing synchronicities.

Synchronicities are the constant trains of thought generated by the consciousness that is The Moment. Since there is nothing but that one consciousness pretending to be the myriad forms of the universe, its thought patterns are manifested in tangible material forms and are expressed as patterns in the world — in music, television shows, things you read, events in your life, connections in your dreams. They can be manifested as, say, a song recurring over and over again throughout the day, a character on a TV show quoting a line from that song, stumbling across a link to that song while reading a news article online — in short, synchronicities are thematic or textual correspondences across all aspects of your life, often communicating something of relevance to you personally. I notice synchronicities constantly, and each time I notice one it tells me I am tuned into existence, I am awake, and I am living in awareness of The Moment.

Synchronicities never stop unfolding around us, but most of us are too lost in the chatter of our inner thoughts to notice them. When your mind is sufficiently still, and when you're attentive to the subtleties of The Moment, you'll begin to observe them.

Observed synchronicities are signs you are living in The Moment actively and consciously. Of course we are always living in The Moment; we can't avoid doing so, since there is nowhere else to be. But living in constant awareness of The Moment is the state mystics have variously called nirvana, satori, moksha, or enlightenment. There's no need to have any particular awareness of The Moment — but that said, there is a great peace to be found in such awareness.

Imagine living with no sense of guilt or isolation, understanding yourself to be that which you see all around you, realizing nothing exists separately from you. This is possible when you come to recognize your true nature.

The Moment is the perfect manifestation of that Consciousness often referred to in limited terms as "God", and you are that consciousness. You are The Moment, along with everything else, seen and unseen, throughout existence. In a sense, anything that happens, "good" or "evil", is done by "God" to "God" — remember, "God" is only pretending that such things as death, evil, shame, guilt, fear, and anger exist. These things, being utterly foreign to that consciousness, are the true miracles of creation, for while The Moment is formed from and animated by the energy of that consciousness, these nonexistent concepts were truly created from nothing at all. They form the heart of The Moment, for without them The Moment would too closely resemble the untroubled ultimate reality native to The Divine, and what would be the point of that? "God" lives in perfect timeless peace, and so The Moment is, to use a crude analogy, "God's" vacation from its normally blissful state.

For this reason, The Moment always appears to be fraught with danger, disappointment, sorrow, loneliness, evil, and death. Just as a movie without a villain is boring, The Moment without the illusion of imminent disaster would be pointless. And so evil, along with all the other unpleasant features of life, is simply the play of "God" pretending to do things to "God", forgetting all the while that it is "God".

All this begs the question: why then should I bother behaving in a moral way? If there are no real consequences, doesn't that mean anything goes…?

*It does seem like you're saying anything goes. But what about evil? Surely you're not saying evil doesn't matter?*

Evil is an illusion of The Moment, contained entirely *within* The Moment. Yes, evil exists, but its nature and its significance are misunderstood. Artfully so, by design.

Without evil, loneliness, death, and the myriad other negative aspects of life, The Moment would be pointless. Since evil and death do not really exist for a timeless singular consciousness — after all, who else would it be evil to? And without time how could death occur? — evil and death are the essential novelties that make The Moment such a compelling experience!

The Moment is, in a loose sense, a vacation the eternal takes from perfection.

## *Then it makes no difference whether I'm good or evil?*

To the Divine Consciousness it makes no difference, no. Those who perpetrate evil are serving their purpose just as perfectly as those who raise children or plant crops or take care of animals. Nothing contained within The Moment penetrates to or has any lasting impact on The Divine. Nothing that happens in this manifested bubble of time has any meaning whatsoever beyond the sheer joy of manifestation. An analogy within The Moment would be listening to music — what is the point of listening to music? What is the aim, and what the consequence? There is no meaning in music beyond the music itself. There can be meaning in lyrics, but the music itself is always simply an experience — a feeling, a moment — with no literal meaning. It is precisely and only itself, and can be enjoyed or rejected only for what it is. There is no point in listening to it beyond listening to it. There may be health benefits, side effects of relaxation or inspiration that motivate someone to listen to a particular piece, but in general there is no aim to listening to music, nothing to be gained or lost, beyond sheer enjoyment that can't really be put into words.

Similarly, beyond the experience of The Moment itself, The Moment has no larger meaning. There is nothing to win or lose in The Moment. The Moment is the point of The Moment. All dualities in The Moment — hot or cold, dark or light, big or small, good or evil — are equally essential and indivisible from the whole.

# *Then why shouldn't I be evil?*

Those who perpetrate evil do so to their detriment. Evil has consequences. Those consequences are confined to The Moment, but since we all live in The Moment, that realization doesn't help us much. The consequences of evil are instantaneous and unavoidable within The Moment — *but only within it.*

There is no "hell", or judgment by a wrathful "God". This concept of judgment is based on a strange circular logic that begins its spiral with the concept of "free will". "God" demands that you be good, and grants you the free will to determine if you will comply with that demand...but if you're good only because there's a cosmic referee who will invariably punish you if you're bad, then how can you truly be good? You can obey, you can conform, you can cower...but how can you be *good*? In the same way, to use an extreme example (as we philosophers are wont to do to make our point), say a rapist is pointing a gun at his victim's head. Under that circumstance, how could the victim ever be said to be consenting to the rape? The victim can choose to keep living and so be raped, but that is not *consent*, that is *acquiescence*. Free will is nothing but a sad farce if one of your two "choices" is certain to incur punishment from an all-powerful judge. The ideas of free will, good and evil, and a tyrannical "God" exacting certain punishment for transgressions are ideas that could never fit together into a coherent whole. This is not the nature of reality.

Good and evil are both concepts entirely confined to The Moment, and The Moment is nothing but the play of The Divine. Being an avatar of The Divine yourself, you are serving perfectly exactly as you are simply by being yourself, no matter what you do — but that said, The Divine doesn't care if you serve perfectly being happy, or being miserable. Your seemingly individual actions do have seemingly individual consequences…but only within The Moment.

The consequence of committing evil is the impact it has on your own experience. That impact is what I call Karmic Gravity.

Karma is an erroneous concept that originated in the Hindu tradition and subsequently permeated Eastern culture. It is the idea that the deeds you do now will impact you, for good or ill, in your next life when you are reincarnated. There are two problems with this idea: there is no separate "you" to be reincarnated, and ideas of good and evil are human concepts with no basis in natural law. Reincarnation is an accurate concept in that since you *are* The Moment, when you "die" every subsequent "birth" is in a sense your reincarnation (though in another sense that birth is *not* your reincarnation since you never went away). But the seemingly separate portion of consciousness that thinks of itself as "you" — the isolated ego containing your memories, preferences, and feelings — does not return from death in some kind of continuous line of existence. What would be the point?

In its true original meaning, karma translates roughly as "action", or "doing". Thus when something happened to you it was said to be your karma, your doing, you being the entirety of action in the nondual universe. In that sense, everything is indeed your doing. But the commonly used concept of karma is based on the notion that individual souls have come here to be perfected, to eventually arrive at some kind of neutral karmic balance that will result in that soul being taken off the "wheel of life", the cycle of birth-death-reincarnation. This idea implies that there are right actions and wrong actions in The Moment — actions *separate* from The Moment, created by independent actors who will subsequently be blessed with good karma or cursed with bad karma. This is not the case — we can't do anything that is independent of The Moment, because it's a nondual process unfolding, and we are that unfolding. No one acts alone on other isolated objects, so no one is functioning better or worse than anyone else. We all serve perfectly by being ourselves, by being unique windows through which The Divine admires itself — this is the unfolding of The Moment.  There is nothing to perfect, nothing to achieve, nowhere we must go, nothing we must do.

Reincarnation is a mistaken notion born of wishful thinking, the idea of life after death.  In reality, there is no death.  A wave that sinks back into the ocean does not die, after all — the ocean *is* the wave.  The wave was not an isolated entity coming into being and then leaving existence, but a change in the state of the ocean that surged and moved as a manifestation of that ocean process.  Once the ocean manifested differently, the wave was absorbed back into the ocean, but it was not obliterated from existence!  A wave that sinks back into the ocean is not lost, nor is it reincarnated in the next wave that follows it; rather, the ocean has never ceased to be.  Its nature is constant flux, change and motion, and whether covered with waves or smooth as glass, it is behaving in a manner consistent with its nature.

So are we all waves in The Moment, surging into manifestation, then merging back into our Source. Nothing that we were is lost except the illusion of ourselves as separate perishable egos; The Divine reincorporates us entirely, for what is there of us separate from The Divine that could be lost in the process?  We are not forgotten, and given that time is an illusion of The Moment, it is conceivable that there will never be a time when we don't exist.

So while karma as a mechanism for justice in the next life doesn't exist, karma does impact us automatically, in this lifetime, without fail and instantaneously. This is the natural law of Karmic Gravity.

# *How does Karmic Gravity work?*

To this point we've focused on the ultimate nature of The Moment rather than the illusory condition that is daily life, the experience most of us have of being separate operators in a world of seemingly separate objects. In discussing The Moment as a nondual unfolding in which all myriad actions are in reality only one constant action, we may seem to be threatening the established moral order. Knowing that you do nothing as an individual actor begs the question: why be moral? If there's no difference between good and evil, why fret about it? Since nothing I do matters, I can do anything I want and blame it on The Moment, right?

In an ultimate sense that's true...but most of us do not live in constant perfect awareness of The Moment. For anyone who did live in that perfect awareness, the question of morality would become moot — in perfect harmony with The Moment, understanding that everyone and everything is "you", the myopic desire to do yourself good at the expense of "another" would vanish, your true divine nature would come to the fore, and you would be overwhelmed by the joy of manifestation, consumed by the wonder of such simple things as motion, and light, and vision, and sound. You would be, as The Divine is, drunk with the wonder of it all.

But most of us will never get to that point, nor should we particularly want to. By the time you finish reading this book, you'll understand that we serve as perfectly in our ignorance as we do in our wisdom. And so the question remains — why be moral?

While it's true in a final sense that good and evil are dualistic divisions having no reality outside of The Moment, we're all pretty much stuck in here with good and evil bouncing around, so we have to deal with them. We still have to go to work in the morning, lock our doors to keep burglars out, avoid pissing off the neighbors, and watch out for muggers in darkened parking lots. Most of us, even as we learn about The Moment and internalize it in our lives, will still go on thinking of ourselves as living in a world of separate objects, acting on those objects and, from time to time, getting kicked in the ass by them. And so, as a practical matter, it behooves us to discuss the law of Karmic Gravity. (Please note that I must now speak in very conventional terms, discussing the idea of separate doers committing good and evil acts as if that notion were true. I am not contradicting myself in this — that idea remains entirely mistaken — but to discuss the illusions of evil and consequence, we have to entertain illusory concepts we know to be inaccurate as if they were actual, solely for the sake of argument. Please bear with me.)

In the *Star Trek* episode *Court Martial*, Mr. Spock said: "If I let go of a hammer on a planet that has a positive gravity, I need not see it fall to know that it has in fact fallen." Gravity is a constant and unavoidable force in the universe correlating to mass; Karmic Gravity is the equally inexorable way that our "individual actions" instantly impact us, for "good" or "ill", while we operate *in* The Moment under the delusion that we are separate *from* The Moment.

Karmic Gravity is entirely confined to The Moment. The Divine is not affected by anything that happens in The Moment; to The Divine, The Moment is somewhat akin to a film so compelling it makes the audience entirely forget they're in a theater. Despite how absorbing manifestation is, the experience of existence has no impact on The Divine. All consequences associated with manifestation are experienced solely within The Moment itself. That said, because we are manifested as The Moment, we do suffer the consequences of "our actions" in The Moment. Though we are not the actors who instigate action, for none of us are agents separate from the nondual Moment, when we are involved in the commission of evil actions we limit the richness of our experience as human beings. This is Karmic Gravity.

The Divine doesn't care if you are playing as Jack the Ripper or Josef Stalin, since for The Moment to work there must be evil, misery and pain as part of its unfolding. That said, when you commit evil, your experience of The Moment as an illusory individual will inevitably be uglier, meaner, and more impoverished than the experience of those who approach The Moment from positions of compassion, charity, and kindness. This is not "divine punishment". This is simply an innate feature of The Moment.

Most instances of evil are fairly petty. They do have consequences, but those consequences are generally proportional to the nature of the act. Tell a lie at work, for example, and the action of Karmic Gravity may be all but imperceptible — your peace of mind will be disturbed to the extent that you have to remember to perpetuate the lie if the topic comes up again...you have to remember you lied to this particular person, and be ever so slightly on guard around that person lest the subject come up again. If you steal a neighbor's newspaper, a part of you may worry the rest of the day that someone else in the neighborhood saw you do it, and then your peace of mind will be disturbed by the notion that some neighbor may now be thinking badly of you, or even spreading gossip about you to the other neighbors. This loss of peace of mind is Karmic Gravity, the unavoidable consequence of a negative action.

Although people seemingly "get away with" corrupt and criminal acts every day, the effects of Karmic Gravity are inescapable. Even when no one is in any position to punish you for your deeds, you're always called to account by your own inner judge, who is constantly aware of your "transgressions". This inner judge is that part of your ego structure that has internalized the rules and values of your culture. You may not even consciously believe in those rules or values anymore, but regardless of your acceptance or rejection of those standards, they exist for most of us as unspoken metrics of behavior against which we constantly measure ourselves. We are raised from the earliest age to accept these notions without question. They are deeply programmed into our core behavioral codes, and run in the background of our awareness like a subroutine, or a virus. Ask yourself this: if you see a young man knock an old woman to the ground, kick her in the head, spit on her, and then steal her purse, how many norms of behavior have been violated in those few seconds? How does even reading that sentence make you feel? And how would you feel if someone falsely accused you of these acts?

Most people will have some emotional revulsion, however slight, at entertaining such a scenario, and even those that have no emotional reaction whatsoever have enough awareness to understand these things are considered wrong by the law specifically and by society universally. So when you transgress against the internalized standards of accepted behavior, even if your conscience doesn't disturb you, your fear of being caught will. (Psychopaths present a different problem, but they don't escape Karmic Gravity either...we'll discuss why momentarily.)

To continue our stolen newspaper example, let's say even though you worry about getting caught, you manage to come up with some kind of rationalization to placate your conscience. Even if your inner judge gives you a pass, reasoning you were right to steal the neighbor's newspaper because he lets his dog poop on your lawn, nevertheless you will still be troubled by the niggling possibility that the snoop across the street might've been peeking through the blinds at you as you stole the paper...that damn dog next door started barking, after all...did I see the blinds move? Dammit, maybe I should put it back *ASAP*...

And so your mind will race. Depending on how neurotic you are, Karmic Gravity may hit you even harder...you may become obsessed with the idea that you've been busted by your snooping neighbor. You may worry about it all weekend, may even be compelled to look for an excuse to talk to the neighbors casually, to try and suss out if any of them suspect you. This is the action of Karmic Gravity.

More serious crimes like bank robbery or murder will impact your peace of mind all the more. Now any time you hear police sirens your heart will quicken just a bit — *are they after me? Have I been found out?* At night you may run through the crime over and over in your mind...*I was careful, wasn't I? I wore a mask...but was some of my hair sticking out in the back? Do they know my hair color now? And my voice when I asked for the money...how distinctive will it be on the security footage? Are the cops just playing dumb, waiting to bust me at any time? Are they closing in on me even now...?*

These self-inflicted thought patterns are only one form of Karmic Gravity; this natural process can also have an insidious impact on one's view of the world. Violent criminals, intimately knowing the ways of violence, will always be somewhat on guard lest violence be perpetrated against them. Dishonest men will inevitably live their lives burdened by the suspicion that someone is cheating them. Thieves must always fret over about the security of their own homes, since they know how easily houses can be burgled.

Contrast these instances with someone who lives his life openly, giving of himself by doing charity work, donating money to homeless people on the streets, feeding stray animals, dealing honestly with everyone and harming no one...how much energy would such a person save, not having to worry about running afoul of the law, the judgment of his peers, or the pangs of his own conscience?  This is, of course, no guarantee that harm will not befall such a person; random acts of misfortune — natural, accidental, or criminal — do occur in The Moment, but such a person is at least not subject to the self-inflicted wounds of Karmic Gravity.  In this way Karmic Gravity is like worry; when we worry about the possibility of future disasters, in a sense we suffer from those future disasters even before they happen. We visualize the imaginary misfortune, our stomach gets upset, we lose sleep, we get nervous...*all over something that is completely imaginary!*  Karmic Gravity is such a self-inflicted wound, the loss of peace of mind that comes with evil.  A "virtuous" person, to the degree that he has nothing to hide and has done no evil, will suffer a lesser degree of self-inflicted fear, guilt, and misery than someone who spends his life harming others.

I had a friend who was raised a devout Catholic, steeped in the notion that God will surely punish the guilty.  In a bar over drinks, I attempted to explain Karmic Gravity to him.  He was quite troubled by the notion.

"There has to be punishment," he protested. "The guilty must suffer!"

"Karmic Gravity *is* suffering," I insisted.  "It may be self-inflicted, but the suffering feels identical to punishment." He shook his head.

"But what about a psychopath? Someone who has no feelings? They're not punished at all, they don't feel a thing! Where's the justice in that?"

I laughed at his righteous need to see punishment inflicted. But even more, I laughed at the assertion that the psychopath, the serial killer, the Maos and the Stalins, escape the consequences of their evil. Karmic Gravity strikes them as well, but in a different way.

The "punishment" for being a psychopath is being a psychopath. That is "punishment" enough, for the psychopath's experience of The Moment is truncated from the start. How much of the richness of life does one miss out on by having no feelings? By never loving, never fearing, never crying...how much of the rich tapestry of life is such a poor wretch denied? This is Karmic Gravity, inescapable and inexorable.

What of Hitler? To do the things he did, a part of you must necessarily be dead — numbed into nonexistence. You cannot commit atrocities, on whatever scale, and remain a complete person. Hitler's sense of empathy would have to be exterminated along with his victims. He would necessarily exist in a cold world of his own making. Even had he conquered all of Europe, inwardly Hitler would be crippled, blind to the rich tapestry of existence, perceiving only those tattered threads of hatred, rage, grievance, and suspicion left in his butchered inner fabric. This is Karmic Gravity.

Similarly, take the case of an Iraqi torturer under Saddam Hussein, an interrogator who one day tortures a little girl in front of her parents, two political enemies of the regime. Suppose (and this is a horrific example, but one must occasionally go to extremes in philosophical arguments to convey the point most clearly) that in the course of the torture the torturer cuts the child's fingers off. Do you suppose this torturer, though escaping justice (for there was no justice in Hussein's regime), would escape this atrocity unscathed? To even commit such a heinous act, a person must numb essential parts of himself within. Truncate parts of himself. Butcher his humanity and bury the severed pieces along with those fingers. Even if the torturer doesn't realize the harm he has done himself, the harm is there. He may not feel it...but there's no way a person like that can see The Moment in the same kind, loving, benevolent way that a normal person sees it. If nothing else, he will never be able to hold his own daughter's hand again without knowing how easily those little fingers can be detached.

A grotesque example, yes, but it aptly illustrates the extreme ways that Karmic Gravity works.

Naturally, my friend was offended by the idea!

"But a psychopath won't know what he's missing! Since he's never known what love is, he won't miss the fact that he can't love! *What good is punishment if he doesn't know he's being punished?*"

Ah, the devout religious thirst for retribution!

The fact is, Karmic Gravity is not punishment. There is no "God" leveling a divine punishment against evil-doers. The evil-doers *are* "God", pretending to do evil *to* "God". There is nothing to be punished, for The Moment is unfolding perfectly, exactly as intended. No...Karmic Gravity is simply an inevitable feature of The Moment, like gravity. Drop a hammer, and it falls. Commit evil, and suffer consequences — not metaphysically for all Eternity in Hell, but now, immediately. You impoverish yourself and your experience of The Moment when you act in negative and harmful ways. This impoverishment may be subjective and self-inflicted, or it may be objective and overt, resulting in beatings, imprisonment, or ultimately execution. It may result in a life of loneliness, despair, or even suicide, but regardless of how it manifests within The Moment, Karmic Gravity is the inevitable consequence that follows hard on the heels of evil.

It is not punishment, so it doesn't really matter whether you recognize your poverty of spirit or not; when you commit evil, depending on the severity of the act, the impact will range from loss of peace of mind to a violent truncation of your experience of The Moment.

Similarly, Karmic Gravity can operate as a form of synchronicity, though it does not always do so. In the same way that thoughts follow like thoughts in the stream of consciousness, actions of a certain character can lead to similar actions in the stream of manifestation. Just as gamblers can get sucked into losing streaks, so too can people be drawn into whirlpools of manifestation, negative thoughts and actions leading to further negative correspondences, resulting in that famous downward spiral Poe referred to in *The Raven* as the fate of that "unhappy master whom unmerciful Disaster followed fast and followed faster". These phenomenal loops can develop, though their exact mechanism is not understood. Obviously there are a lot of weasels running around out in the world, getting away with all sorts of rotten things. If this kind of downward spiral were directly correlated to a certain concentration of evil actions, we'd see an awful lot of corrupt politicians spontaneously bursting into flames! That we do not observe this indicates that, while Karmic Gravity is inevitable, it does not always condense into a downward spiral.

# *What about justice for those who are wronged?*

There's no need for justice, since there's no such thing as injustice. All things that happen begin and end with The Divine manifesting The Moment, and as such, all things are perfect. Things perceived as injustices are committed by The Divine on The Divine, and it is The Divine that, forgetting itself, seeks retribution — though only when laboring under the willful delusion that something bad has happened, that there was a victim and a perpetrator, and that there is something to avenge.

I'm speaking from an ultimate perspective here, In terms of our daily lives and the viability of our civilization, we should not hesitate to enforce our laws and punish wrongdoers. Inflicting retribution on criminals is not inconsistent with The Moment — indeed, busting bad guys is as much a part of this game of existence as listening to soft classical music, or contemplating wisdom while writing haiku in the presence of wind chimes! Realization of The Moment cannot even be properly said to be a pacifistic philosophy, since whether or not we execute death row prisoners is of no importance to The Divine or The Moment...though such executions will have consequences of Karmic Gravity on the individuals, and perhaps the society, implementing them. That said, executing prisoners is as much a part of The Moment as holding a newborn baby or watching a sunset...without punishment, after all, how would we ever know the quality of mercy?

But in an ultimate metaphysical sense, there is no need for justice. The Moment is nothing more than a playground for The Divine. It is unbearably sad, filled with danger, riddled with evil, plagued by injustice, choked by hate...and none of these things at all.

At the same time, all of these nonexistent woes are indispensable to The Moment. Without them, The Moment would resemble the unperturbed natural state of The Divine...and then what would be the point?

Without the illusion of imminent disaster, The Moment would be a pretty pointless vacation, and The Divine might as well have stayed home.

## *What is my purpose?*

To be yourself. The Moment is an expression of The Divine created so it may experience itself as all the things it is not — separate, bound by time and space, finite, and existing in complete uncertainty.

The Divine has manifested itself as you.

It has done so for two reasons: to confront other aspects of itself through you, and to behold this astonishing creation from your unique point of view. In all of creation, you are the only viewpoint that experiences and perceives The Moment in your particular way, from your exact vantage point in the universe, through the filter of your unique experience. Your memories, triumphs, fears, delusions, insecurities, moments of transcendent joy, moments of utter despair — these are your reasons for being.

There is no one in The Moment who is, or has been, or ever will be, exactly like you. Only you can provide The Divine with your singular experience of The Moment. You are therefore irreplaceable and essential, as much as anything or anyone that exists or has ever existed. Between you and the Buddha there is no distance. You are as loved and vital as Christ, as

Gandhi, as Krishna. "God" sees through your eyes, listens through your ears, feels the kiss of his breeze on your skin, thinks through your thoughts, loves with your heart. Therefore, your purpose is simply to be yourself, however you are.

It's that simple. You have no need to do anything in particular, certainly no need to improve yourself. As imperfect and flawed as you think yourself to be, you have no higher purpose than to be yourself.

And you fulfill your purpose perfectly. Always.

*"The Sage does less and less every day until he does nothing at all, and then nothing is left undone."*
*You said this earlier...what does it mean?*

You are not the doer of deeds. The idea that "I" "do" "actions" is a linguistic conceit. When an event occurs, it is not the result of a cause, but the fluctuation of one process. There is no separate "I" capable of acting on a separate "that". There is one consciousness underlying everything. A fire is the air and the wood, as much as the flames and the hand that set it. A shooting star is simultaneously the meteorite headed for Earth, the atmosphere resisting it, the gravity pulling it down, the space through which it falls, the flames as it burns, and the mind that perceives it, that bit of consciousness that tracks its movement across the sky and formulates the thought: "A shooting star...I must make a wish".

The Sage, the enlightened master, realizes more and more as time "passes" that he is not the source of action, the initiator of phenomena, but rather the phenomenon itself. He does not originate actions, but participates in them. After all, when you score a goal in a soccer game, you could not kick that ball unless someone had made the ball. Furthermore, you couldn't kick the ball and score unless someone had invented the game (for while you can kick a ball into a net while practicing, you can't actually score except in the context of a game). Furthermore, you couldn't score a goal in the absence of basic survival prerequisites like sunlight to provide warmth, air to breathe, ground to play on…you couldn't score a goal without gravity, without the electromagnetic field shielding the Earth from radiation, without the activity of the quantum strings that form matter and energy, without the unified field from which strings and universes emerge…

The Sage lives in an awareness of The Moment that is larger than his illusory sense of separateness. He realizes, more and more every day, that he is not the actor but the act. His knowledge deepens until he finally realizes that he does not act at all because he is not separate from anything and is himself the unfolding of The Moment. At that point, he no longer suffers from guilt, or fear, or envy…or for that matter, pride, or ego, or merit. He is not responsible for anything that happens as an actor isolated from the process.

At that point, he realizes The Moment is sufficient in itself. He has no need to act, and indeed *cannot* act autonomously, but only in concert with the entirety of The Moment, and at that point he rests secure in his knowledge that he is free of responsibility…at that point he knows nothing remains for him to do, for he was never doing anything by himself. He finally knows that The Moment unfolds as it will, and at that point he realizes that nothing needs to be done, and so nothing is left undone.

The Moment is perfect as it is, regardless of what he does or doesn't do; it always was, and it always will be. Even so, we tend to see action in a very simplistic and limited way. When we hear "you are not the doer of deeds", the egocentric viewpoint within us rebels against the notion. By way of example, let's examine a hypothetical, the case of a woman being told that she is not the source of her actions.

"I am a single mother with two kids...I have to work twelve hours a day at two jobs just to put food on the table. How dare you say I'm not doing anything, that if I just understand this "Moment" of yours then nothing will be left undone! Of course I act! I act every day to take care of my kids, and I work hard at it too!"

To her I would reply: of course we participate in action in the world. We are always engaged in action, even when we sit still, even when we sleep, for even asleep our brains are still active, we still breathe, our hearts continue to beat, the particle fields that form our bodies, along with the entire universe, continue to oscillate...but it is the nature of action that is misunderstood. We do not engage in action in the sense of instigating action solely by our own volition; rather, acts occur that occur concurrently *with* us.

The mother that works two jobs to support her kids believes herself responsible for her actions, but fails to see that The Moment is not only the author of her situation, but also the author of her response to her situation.

Her every action is really an incalculably vast network of interactions. For the situation incorporating her action to occur, this woman had to meet a man and create children with him. For her to become a single mother, the father had to disappear, for whatever reason; likewise, her children had to survive childbirth. Likewise, in order for this state of affairs to exist, this woman must have been raised with a moral code — a sense of responsibility and industriousness — sufficient to prevent her from acting solely in her own pragmatic self-interest, say having an abortion, giving the kids up for adoption, or simply abandoning them. This code would have to be strong enough to sustain her self-sacrifice through difficult times, even as she works herself ragged for their benefit.

She thinks she has a choice, that she has *decided* to behave as she does, but the truth is The Moment has unfolded in this way, and she is inextricably woven into the fabric of The Moment. All these circumstances had to occur to lead to the point where her action — working two jobs to support two kids alone — could even be possible. "She" had no control over these factors. Furthermore, to act as she does, she must have certain innate characteristics and drives — a sense of responsibility, the ability to love, the ability to care more for others than for herself, the ability to focus effort. Without these qualities, she could not execute these actions…or rather, these actions would not occur with her participation in them.

How did she come to have these characteristics? Did any of us start life with a checklist, choosing this or that attribute to have ingrained within us? Of course not. If she has a sense of morality, it is not only because she was born with an inner capacity to process and internalize moral concepts, it also means she was raised by someone who taught her right from wrong (from their point of view, of course), and gave her enough love to ensure she was not emotionally stunted and capable herself of receiving and giving love; again, she had no choice in how she was formed, or how her parents raised her.

To turn out as she did, she had to have a relatively normal and undamaged brain, a brain capable of experiencing emotions (psychopaths are not so lucky), a brain that can retain memories and enable her to be sufficiently intelligent to handle the logistical challenges of two jobs with two children — again, the quality of her brain was not her doing.

To "perform the actions" she does, she had to have life experiences that made her resilient enough to cope with such a challenging situation; obviously, a spoiled child with a pampered early life might well lack the grit to struggle daily in such a relentless way.

In all of these considerations, this woman cannot be said to be the author of her own nature and her position in life unless she was entirely in control of everything that happened to her, not only her physical attributes from birth, but how her parents raised her, and everything that subsequently happened to her in life. None of us wield such control...so why this persistent illusion that we are isolated autonomous entities that act separately? And why this crushing sense that we are responsible for the world?

Within the context of this matrix, let's consider the issue of individual choice. Given all these circumstances (and countless other factors interacting with her constantly, many of them beneath the threshold of conscious perception), our hypothetical single mother has no choice but to act as she does. She *thinks* she could act differently — she could leave her kids, she could give them up for adoption, she could get married and send them to boarding school, she could kill herself, kill them — because all those alternatives are physically possible. They are alternatives she is physically capable of implementing, yes...but in reality, given how The Moment has unfolded, her personality, her sense of morality, how endearing her kids are, the marital opportunities or lack thereof at hand, she has no real choice in how she acts — *that sense of choice is an illusion.*

Where her children are concerned, she will always choose self-sacrifice and love without fail because that's how she is manifested in The Moment. She is not acting on her own because she has no volition, no real choice. She is neither to credit nor to blame. If she had been raped and impregnated at the age of fifteen, for example, this situation could have been far different. She might have been so traumatized by the crime and subsequent pregnancy that she would no longer be open to having kids. She might have had her tubes tied, or had an abortion and then been damaged by the procedure, physically or emotionally. Or if she were born a lesbian, she would not be raising two kids alone...certainly not these two kids, not by that same father. Our seeming actions are a complex matrix of interlocking circumstances over which we have no direct control; indeed, rather than being separate static individuals isolated from the world by barriers of skin, we are like whirlpools of intersecting currents and materials, none of which we personally direct or engineer. So the question remains: why do we feel so responsible for our deeds?

To use a much simpler example: I'm a huge fan of the movie *Forbidden Planet*, and have an obsession with

Robby the Robot. I have, from time to time, seen a full-sized exact reproduction of Robby the Robot, complete with lights and animated head, on sale in various high-end catalogs for $10,000. I can't afford that...and yet I still lust after that robot. Why I can't say...the way I've unfolded in The Moment, I'm the kind of guy that freaks out over geeky things. I grew up on comics and Star Trek, I love robots and toys, and I always will.

So that said, if someone walked up to me and said "I will sell you a life-sized Robby the Robot for a thousand dollars," I would not be able to resist. I would buy it every single time *if there were any possible way I could swing it, regardless of the consequences.* Understand, it's not like I can afford a thousand dollars either...but there's room on a credit card for that amount. My wife would be angry indeed, justifiably so given how much we've struggled to pay off the credit cards. But regardless, even if the circumstances were such that she'd be furious with me, in that instant I would get out that credit card and buy that Robby. Only serious practical circumstances would prevent me from buying it: if I didn't have room on a card, if we were literally starving-level broke, if we were in the midst of an expensive medical treatment...but that's not saying anything I haven't said. If The Moment unfolded in a way that it was at all possible, regardless of the consequences, I would have no choice but to buy that robot.

Similarly, I love animals. And so no matter what else I'm doing in my life, if a cat or other animal comes to my door in need, I will feed and water that animal. If it will let me pet it, I will pet it. And knowing everything that I know about the perfection of The Moment, when I see a dead animal on the side of the road I will always feel a momentary sadness before my awareness of that perfection returns. Perhaps one day my understanding of The Moment will be such that no calamity can even momentarily impact it...but I'm not at that exalted place yet. Nor do I particularly care anymore if I get there, because the perfection of The Moment would not be impacted by my level of awareness in the slightest; that said, even if I ever do embody that perfect awareness, I will still feed stray animals. Even though I know whatever happens to them is perfectly okay, I will still always choose to feed them. This is neither a merit nor a flaw. This is simply me being me.

Due to my awareness of The Moment, I accept myself as I am, for my state is always in harmony with The Moment, no matter what I'm doing. That self-acceptance of my nature is the kind of wisdom I hope to impart to you with this book. The point is not to be "perfect", dwelling in a constant blissful awareness of The Moment (it's possible, but rare). The greatest acceptance you can come to is the acceptance of yourself *exactly as you are*. To be aware that your manifestation includes your self-perceived flaws, that without those flaws you would not be yourself, and without you as you are right now The Moment would be deprived of your unique viewpoint...that is the highest wisdom.

It took me many a dark night of the soul to finally accept that even as I am — overly sentimental, enslaved by small animals, too fond of craft cocktails for my own good, often impatient, insufferably arrogant, masochistically self-deprecating, frequently resentful, occasionally angry, sporadically foolish, and perpetually lusting after Robby the Robot for reasons beyond my ken (other than "he's so cool") — despite all of that, I am perfectly in The Moment. When you can know yourself as The Moment, all difficulties disappear. Just with that acceptance of yourself — and along with yourself, The Moment — you are in harmony with all of existence, no matter where you go or what you do.

The difference between living in perfect awareness of The Moment and living a typically ignorant life is not the difference between perfection and imperfection. In the former case, you live in constant awareness that whatever happens is ultimately okay, loving your enemies as you love yourself because they are, in every single instance, you. In the latter case, you're normal. And in both cases you're perfectly fine.

We are the action, not the actors. Free will and choice seem to be ours, but in truth The Moment unfolds and we are The Moment. We act as we are, but we do not choose who we are, or what conditions for action spring up around us — we just are.

To some this may seem a bleak prospect, the notion that we are all just puppets, devoid of free choice, dancing our predetermined moves in a choreographed simulation of life. That would be true if we consider The Divine to be some kind of puppet master foreign to us, calling all the shots in The Moment like the Wizard of Oz behind his curtain...but this is not the case.

The glory of The Moment is that we *are* The Divine. We *are* The Moment. We *do* act...not as tiny isolated individuals, but as the entirety of creation! Does our hypothetical mother work two jobs while raising two kids? Certainly in a sense she does...but she is also the kids she is raising, and the movement of clouds above her head, the rainbow after it rains in her yard, and the stars shining above her little house. She does — we do — so much more than the tiny details of our little lives. We are endless, we are grand, and that which we do is inexpressibly perfect. Look around...that flock of birds moving across the sky like curls of black smoke, weaving spirals and lines across the clouds...that's your doing. That is The Moment unfolding in all its splendor, and that is you.

One rainy winter morning I was looking out my window into the yard. There I saw a little gray dove on the wet ground, hopping lightly from fallen branch to fallen branch, seemingly oblivious to the cold and rain, bobbing its head here and there, eating bugs. It didn't hesitate at any point, did not seem to dwell at all on the weather, or the bugs...it saw a bug, it ate a bug, and moved on.

I found the bird's "actions" to be a very interesting contrast to my own "actions". In general, when I find a bug in my house, I will go to some effort to capture it and put it outside, because I recognize the divinity of the bug as I recognize my own, and so I feel compelled to put it safely outside rather than kill it. And yet, here was this dove in the cold rain, killing bugs without hesitation or reflection, existing perfectly in The Moment, without a care beyond the immediacy of its experience now, untroubled by so-called higher thoughts or conscience, killing without hesitation the bugs I laboriously put outside. This further led me to an odd thought: my supposed good deed, putting bugs outside, could be a very bad deed for other bugs when that bug happens to be a spider, because then every poor insect that spider eats is on my head, isn't it? After all, it was in my house and I put it outside, so every bug it eats from that point on is my doing. Indeed, the very bugs I put outside, meaning to do them well, I may be delivering into the fangs of the very spider I put outside last week!

This illustrates the mistaken ideas that we act independently, that we are responsible for the outcomes of our actions, and that benefit can exist separately from detriment. All our seemingly separate actions, no matter how well-intentioned, are beneficial to some, and detrimental to others.

When we get a job, we help ourselves and our families at the expense of all the others who didn't get the job. Plant a tree, and harm the grasses and weeds that will eventually be starved of sunlight in its shade. Feed a feral pregnant cat, and you may be condemning her kittens down the line to abandonment and starvation. Likewise, bad actions may lead to positive results. An example of this is the tale of the young man in ancient China who broke his leg — surely a misfortune if ever there was one! And yet a week later the local warlord sent his troops into the young man's village to draft all able-bodied men into military service. Because the young man had a broken leg, they left him in the village, and he was spared the horrors of war.

Even when we erroneously think of action in terms of cause and effect, we must admit there's no way for us to anticipate what effects will arise from our causes. A harsh word to someone may hurt them, or it may lead them to a self-examination that will deliver them from some delusion. A neighbor of mine put an old television out on the curb with a note saying "Free TV, works fine". I noticed this on a Friday. Over the weekend it rained. On Monday I noticed it was still sitting outside. It occurred to me that if someone took that TV home now and plugged it in, it might still have rain water in it. It might cause a fire, or deliver someone a terrible electric shock. Yet was this television a clever assassination attempt by a hostile neighbor? Or simply a charitable gesture, thoughtlessly delivered?

I tell you this not to convince you of the futility of engaging in action, not to get you to refrain from acting and withdraw from the world (as if you could do either...no matter where you go, there you are...), but to loosen your grip on the delusion of being in control of anything. Even if you believe yourself to be a separate individual acting in a cause and effect universe, since you cannot foresee the effects of your actions, which will benefit some and harm others, how could you properly claim responsibility for your actions? When you can't control how they turn out and can't foresee whom they may harm?

Instead of feeling responsible for everything in your individual life — guilt for your sins, anger at your limitations, frustration that your desires haven't been fulfilled — you can realize the larger truth, and let go of feeling the weight of your own life on your shoulders. Knowing the ways of The Moment, you can be free to watch it — to watch yourself — unfold, without judgments, without expectations, without fear, without regrets. You can know that The Moment is perfectly fulfilling its purpose, and you perfectly serve The Moment simply by being yourself.

When you understand that you yourself do nothing, then you can at last let go of guilt and anger, envy and fear. You can know that you are the unfolding of The Moment, along with everything else. And you can watch that unfolding without judgments, without assigning blame or merit, secure in the certitude that The Moment needs nothing from you other than you being yourself, providing that invaluable and unique window through which The Divine may regard itself. Then you realize that you do nothing at all, and nothing needs to be done, and nothing is left undone.

*Even knowing this, I still blame myself...all the things I've done, all my failures. I often feel depressed and worthless. How can I stop feeling badly about myself?*

I've spent so much of my life telling myself "you need to be better". When I'd catch myself being selfish, when I'd judge others uncharitably, when I'd hurt other people to further my own desires, I'd feel badly and resolve to myself "you need to be better".

It took me all these years of study, writing, and reflection to finally realize that whenever I said "you need to be better", I was really saying "you need to be better than you *are*". Only then did I realize how futile this desire was. It's exactly like saying "I need to be taller than I am", or "I need to be smarter than I am". It's like a grasshopper saying "I need to be a lizard", or a tree saying "I need to walk over to that nicer meadow over there".

How can you be other than how you are? If you could be better than you are, then you *would already be better than you are*. (I'm not talking about skills here...obviously practicing playing the piano can make you a better piano player; in this I'm speaking about fundamental personal attributes, not acquired skills.)

120

In telling myself "you need to be better", I was really complaining that I wasn't measuring up to my imaginary ideal. All of us have grown up within some kind of conceptual moral framework, with some kind of behavioral yardstick that our parents, our church, and our society expect us to measure up against. As a result, we all have this imaginary ideal version of ourselves in our minds, a perfect "me" that is always patient, never selfish, doesn't lie...indeed, this ideal "me" always copes with problems brilliantly, is never moody, and is largely happy even in the face of adversity.

This ideal "me" is, of course, an unreal construct having nothing whatsoever to do with the reality of The Moment. It presupposes we have a kind of perfect understanding of and control over ourselves, and that when we misbehave we're doing so willfully, allowing our perfect control over ourselves to slip. Clearly this is not the case...it *seems* to be the case because our imaginary ideal self has precisely that level of perfect control...but that imaginary ideal doesn't exist. If I am selfish in The Moment, even against my fervent desire to be generous, how could it be said my selfishness was a choice? If I'm selfish it's because I couldn't help myself. I *would've* done better if I *could've* done better. We think we could have behaved differently...but we are obviously mistaken, since we behaved as we did. Yes, in theory, in accordance with my ideal vision of myself, in practical terms of actual potential I could've behaved differently...I physically *could* have saved the last doughnut for my poor wife, for example...but in reality I *couldn't* have behaved differently because I *didn't* behave differently. By their deeds shall ye know them! In that instant I could not resist eating the last doughnut because my desire for the doughnut was greater than my desire to be selfless. Do I have an internal dial I can use to re-balance myself, to swing my desire between the two conflicting poles to a more desirable setting? *I* certainly don't...and I suspect you don't either. So how could I be better than I actually am?

This holds true for everyone. Even the most evil individuals, possessing no desire to better themselves, are still doing the best they can. They may be so emotionally or spiritually damaged that they can only manifest hostility and hatred, but even then the question remains — *how could they be other than what they are?* How can they better themselves when they're the very selves that need to be bettered?

On the flip side, the idea of gaining merit is equally delusional. How are you to be credited for being yourself? If you work at an animal shelter, or donate to the homeless, it's because you have those capacities in your nature...generosity, strength, kindness. Does that make you superior to one more impoverished than you, who has no such inner resources?

There is no you to be blamed, no you to be lauded, apart from The Moment. Knowing this can also save you the trouble of blaming yourself for not acquiring the merit you think is your due — yet another way that we torment ourselves with imaginary conceits, this idea of "not living up to our potential".

Although there is nothing you need to do, nothing to be gained and nothing to be lost, if you seek greater awareness of The Moment as it actually exists, you would do well to get over this theoretical ideal idea of yourself; it is a fiction, with no more reality than Superman or Santa Claus.

You are not the actor — you are the action. And there is only one action. And that action is The Moment.

*You say I can do nothing wrong, but what does that mean in practical terms when I can ruin my life in an instant, say by robbing a bank, or killing someone?*

In absolute terms, "you" can do no wrong because you do not act as a separate entity. Some of us, manifesting in evil currents, believe ourselves to be performing evil acts under our own power. Even after reading this book, some of you will continue to think that way, and may even be thinking "hey, now I have a license to do whatever I want". As my part of the unfolding of The Moment, I would like to discourage you from gravitating toward evil unfoldings by pointing out the inevitable things that unfold alongside evil — guilt, fear, pain, suffering, and death. There's nothing wrong with these things in an ultimate sense...but they're not much fun to experience in The Moment. If you want your unfolding to be synonymous with suffering and misery, evil's a great way to get you there. Otherwise, your unfolding will be much more pleasant to the degree you steer clear of manifesting evil.

Which leads us to the next question: How can I steer clear of manifesting evil when I do nothing at all? When I'm not even the author of my own actions, what choice do I have in any of this?

This is a very tricky question, given how easy it is to misunderstand the nature of action. One action occurs, and that action is The Moment, yes…but what is actually occurring when "I" "act"?

Think of yourself doing something simple — let's say picking a leaf up off the ground. Even when performing this simple action, you are performing countless actions simultaneously. Your nervous system is processing a dizzying number of neurological transactions, chemical and electrical impulses racing along nerves, signaling muscles all over your body to bend, to extend, to twist, to contract. Flooded by countless sensations — the movement of the air across your skin, the myriad scents in the air, the sounds of the wind, the chirping of birds — you ignore all but the sight of the leaf on the ground, and the activity necessary to grasp it. Beyond this, in every one of your billions of cells, processes are occurring — mitochondria moving about generating energy, lysosomes breaking down waste products, Golgi apparatus synthesizing nutrients. Some of these cells are constantly waging war with hostile invading bacteria and viruses, and on a quantum level, particles in your body, manifested from the same field that manifests those particles across the entirety of creation, vibrate in a frenzied dance of existence. An entire microverse of frantic action underlies even the simplest things you do.

In the same way, The Moment acts, and all the seemingly separate objects and processes that make up the universe are that unified action. So, you ask: how do I avoid committing evil and suffering from Karmic Gravity? If I'm "bad", how can I change?

If you desire to change, that means the entirety of The Moment supports that change and conspired to awaken that awareness within you. If you don't desire to change, that's perfectly fine as we've already discussed. But if you've been involved in evil currents within The Moment and long to break free of them, to manifest differently, then you must realize such change is not only possible, it is already in progress.

You see, this is a seeming problem that is really no problem at all. If the idea of changing your life even occurs to you, it is because in the Now of The Moment you are already manifesting differently. You are, in conceiving of yourself changing, already changing. The thought, the motivation, would never have occurred to you if that were not so.

It's kind of a reverse Catch-22. In *Catch-22*, the classic novel by Joseph Heller, no matter what you tried to do to improve your situation, there was always some regulation in place that would prevent you from succeeding. In this process it's rather the reverse. If you're playing the part of a rotten bastard and you have no desire to change, that's perfectly okay; The Moment needs rotten bastards against which to measure saints. The rotten bastard will suffer, probably in ignorance of why he's suffering, yes...but so what? Without the reality of suffering, there could be, in reality, no joy. The rotten bastard's soul is not at risk since there is only one soul and it's having a marvelous time, so there's no problem there.

But let's say you want to change. This is only a problem if you believe yourself to be a powerless isolated individual who is beset by obstacles to change on all sides, a poor little you that must change, and quickly, entirely under your own poor little power. In other words, you're suffering from delusions that a) you are in need of change and b) you are powerless to change!

In truth, if you find yourself wanting to change, you are already changing, and it is only because the entire universe has aligned to facilitate that change — how's that for a support group?

For example, if in reading this book you've suddenly discovered you want to change your life, where do you think that idea came from? Millions of variables conspired to place this book in your hands *right now*. Think about it — I had to be born, I had to grow up miserable and alienated enough to seek out answers to life's big questions, I had to be intelligent enough to pursue this line of inquiry in seclusion, reading countless books in search of the truth until, not finding any one book that perfectly answered my questions, I decided to write one of my own. After one false start writing an entirely different book, I had to be aware enough to realize that language alone was inadequate to convey ultimate truth. I had to pause, and continue my search for enlightenment not solely through intellect, but through internalizing the immediacy of experience in my gut.

And then, finally, after flailing about, striving to squeeze "the universe into a ball / To roll it towards some overwhelming question", as T.S. Eliot so aptly put it, one morning I had to wake up knowing I would call my book "The Moment", suddenly glimpsing the first stirrings of the deeper enlightenment I'd been searching for most of my life. All that, to put this book into your hands. And only you know all the twists and turns in your life that led you to pick up this book, and read whatever made you realize you want to change.

And so you have changed. That desire to change is change itself, arising as The Moment. And further change will proceed in the same way, as the entirety of creation unfolding in a different way within you and without you.

The desire to change never arises separately from the process of change, for that desire is change itself.

You do not need to understand how to change, you simply need to know that, in desiring to change, that change is already not only possible, but proceeding. Do not interfere in that change with egocentric demands, impatience, judgments, or fear. Watch that change unfold with openness, constant awareness, and patience. Proceed in this way and before you know it, you will *be that change*.

So if, in ignorance, you were manifesting in evil currents of unfolding, your very awareness of that process is itself the process of moving out of those currents into new currents of more benevolent unfolding. Keeping that awareness and desire in the forefront of your mind will further move you into different currents, for just as thoughts follow like thoughts, happenings follow like happenings, and synchronicities follows synchronicities. Your attention coupled with your intention will allow you to unfold in new ways.

It is, and is not, through your own power. Acting under the delusion of being a separate tiny piece of a fractured universe, you are virtually powerless. Knowing yourself as The Moment, the very source of all power and change, you finally realize that the height of glory is being you exactly as you are, and nothing could be more miraculous than the view from your own eyes.

When you can do that, when you can accept yourself as you are, the chief impediment to change — the pressure of feeling that you *must* change — is removed, and so change is free to unfold as it will, unimpeded by ego and fear. More than any other factor, our ego structures get in our way, binding us to old patterns and rigid definitions. Knowing that change has begun to occur the instant the *idea* of change occurs, realizing that change is available but not required, we can allow change to unfold in our lives without impediment.

THE MOMENT

*But is there anything I can do to change myself,
other than just waiting for The Moment to unfold?*

The Moment is constantly changing, and you are The
Moment. At the root of this question there seems to
be a certain impatience — I want to change *now*, so
why can't I just get *on* with it?

You cannot, as a separate individual, change yourself
through your own willpower for the simple reason
that you are not a separate individual! But of course,
people do change. You yourself have no doubt
changed over the course of your life, and though you
may feel yourself to be the author of those changes,
you are not...not as a separate entity apart from
everything else.

For example, let's say you always walk past beggars on
the street without a thought, never giving them so
much as a spare quarter because, let's say for the sake
of argument, "you" are selfish. Then let's say one day
you're walking down the street and you notice an old
lady begging on the corner, and she catches your eye
mainly because she looks a lot like your mother. This
moves you deeply and unexpectedly. You think of
your mother, forced to live homeless on the streets,
and the thought shakes you to the core. You give her
all the money in your wallet that day, and from then

131

on you make it a point to be charitable to homeless people whenever you see them, because you understand them to be human beings now, as opposed to background annoyances beneath your daily radar. You are now less selfish...but is that your doing?

Could that change in you have happened without the entire universe arranging itself, through an inconceivable number of variables, to place a desperate woman resembling your mother in your path, instigating this change in how you, along with the rest of the world, manifest? Or are you really going to claim that la-de-da, just like that, you spontaneously improved yourself and stopped being selfish?

Did Scrooge improve himself? Or did everyone in Charles Dickens' novel — Marley, Tiny Tim, Bob Cratchit, Fezziwig, the three Ghosts of Christmas, and the entire socioeconomic structure of Great Britain in the 19th Century — author his change? Abandon the simplistic notion that you are the author of yourself. In the sense of being a tiny separate thing in a universe of separate things, the idea is laughable. Still, that said, *of course* you are capable of changing. In fact, you can never stop changing even if you try.

People are not static things. We do seemingly change as our lives continue, but we are not the authors of our change, nor do these changes occur "over time". Remember there is no past, no future — how we behave now is the entirety of our behavior. We cannot be other than we are *now*. As Now unfolds, we may act differently under the different circumstances of Now, but we will be no more to credit or blame for "our" actions in *this* configuration of the entire universe than we were when we behaved differently in *that* configuration of the entire universe. In the sense of being The Moment itself, you are of course the author of all change. But in the sense of being a separate isolated ego, all you can do is accept yourself as you are now, with the understanding that now will always change.

That said, remember what we discussed regarding synchronicities and Karmic Gravity. While I hesitate to buy into the whole "law of attraction" concept because I think that idea is too simplistic to be reliably applied in such a complex system, there is something to be said for coordinating changes in your life through applied intentions.

Once you begin focusing on positive thoughts of change, these thoughts will slowly begin leading to other like thoughts. This can foster fundamental changes in your attitude, changes that will reverberate throughout your life. Synchronicities may subsequently materialize, circling you in increasing numbers, encouraging the occurrence of circumstances in keeping with the change you're encouraging through constant awareness.

In some cases this change is relatively simpler to instigate. An alcoholic, for example, has a fairly clear path to change: rehab, abstention, therapy, and support groups, the only impediment being the force of the addiction itself. Deeper fundamental changes in character are more nebulous to visualize and much harder to manifest. Even so, change is not only possible, but inevitable. The challenge is directing that change along desired paths, and avoiding the self-judgment and impatience that can impede that change.

But the best way to create whatever change you desire is simply this: know yourself as The Moment and thereby gain enlightenment.

Opening yourself to The Moment, living in awareness of your unity with all things, can in and of itself radically change your life, in both desired and unexpected ways. For instance, consider the previous example of our hypothetical alcoholic. Let's say that he started drinking, and continues doing so, to mask the pain of childhood abuse. He wants to quit drinking because it's destroying him, but simply abstaining from hitting the bottle isn't going to address the core issue of his pain.

Now consider if this alcoholic were to know The Moment, to understand who he really is, the real nature of action, and the underlying beauty and perfection of this experience we call manifestation. Do you think that realization would make his desired change easier, or harder? If he were to realize The Moment deeply, becoming enlightened in the classic sense, is it hard to see how the emotional anguish motivating his drinking could vanish instantly? He would certainly still face some physical issues from going cold turkey, but the core motivation behind his drinking would dissolve; imagine what knowledge of The Moment would do to his worldview, to his thoughts regarding his abuser, and his image of himself. What do you think this knowledge would mean in terms of any changes you want to make in your life? Certainly, on a superficial level, relieved of the burden of being responsible for changing, and knowing that you have no need to change, change would become much less of a mountain to climb, wouldn't it?

But ever more importantly, isn't it conceivable that all these changes you feel so pressed to make now might no longer seem so important? Of course I'm not speaking of mere physical changes, like exercising more, losing weight, or eating healthier food...I'm speaking now of inward changes...changes in attitude, in awareness, in behavior...those changes we consider "spiritual". If you came to know yourself as The

Moment, mightn't your desire to change vanish altogether? What part of you would still remain that was in need of change?

Isn't it possible, even probable, that knowing yourself as The Moment, you would realize you're fine exactly as you are?

*I hear what you say, but I still feel alone, fearful, stressed. What will happen if I do as you say, if I come to know The Moment in this way?*

Your life will be enormously transformed if you can just stop blaming yourself. Even just that small change would vastly alter your daily experience of everything.

When you're enlightened, you don't have to feel guilty for things you've done anymore. You realize that the unfolding of The Moment is the author of your actions, that The Moment is actually the doing of The Divine, and as such The Moment is in accord, in all respects, with the divine will. Given that you are not the initiator of action but the action itself, all action being in reality the unfolding of The Moment, how are you guilty of anything? And once you realize you don't have to feel guilty for your actions, you can also let go of anger, blame, and resentment toward others for things they've seemingly done to you. Blame is a two-way street. Jesus said: "Judge not, that ye be not judged". It seems evident to me Christ did not mean that God would judge you, but simply that when you judge anyone, you also measure yourself by the same relentless yardstick, whether or not you're aware you're doing so. Most of us inflict judgments and self-recriminations on ourselves constantly every single day. In a sense, self-recrimination is the most persistent form of suffering; no matter what you do, you can never escape the judge that inhabits your own skin.

For the longest time, I hated myself. Literally, there would be moments, every single day, when I would remember a regret over something I'd done or failed to do, recalling a grudge or an opportunity I let slip by, and I would say aloud "I hate myself". Literally say that *aloud*, many times a day, with only myself in the room to hear. Reflexively I would say it, with shame, regret, and disgust. This book was the breakthrough that finally silenced that inner voice and freed me to revel in The Moment. In ordering my thoughts so simply, I could no longer escape the conclusion that The Moment is indeed all that exists. I speak from experience: by knowing the truth of The Moment, you can let go of blame, toward yourself and others. That alone will transform your life, freeing you of all the negative emotions that go along with judging.

The flip side of blame is credit, and both forms of judgment are equally poisonous to true knowledge of The Moment. You are no more to be applauded for the things you've "achieved" than you are to be blamed for your "shortcomings". Knowing the truth of The Moment, you can be free to simply be, without explanation, without any need for justification. You can live your life unburdened by the demands of your ego, accepting yourself entirely as you are — the manifestation of The Divine in time and space. You can let go of the need to achieve anything, let go of feeling disappointed over lost opportunities in the past, let go of the niggling suspicion as you age that you've wasted your life because this goal or that goal was never achieved. You are free to pursue your dreams, or not, without fear of failure. You are free to act without the burden of needing certain results to arise from your action. You can pursue your goals without the crushing need for success. You can act purely for the joy of acting, knowing that whatever you do is in service to The Divine.

When you can accept yourself, you can accept others. When they seemingly wrong you, you can understand they're lost in the illusion of being lone actors responsible for their actions. They feel guilt for the things they've done, they're fearful, they're angry at others for things done to them, they lash out at you for their own misguided reasons, all because they don't understand The Moment.

When you gain knowledge of The Moment, you naturally embody a deep love of and compassion for all of creation. But this compassion can exist in you without sorrow. When you encounter one in need you are free to help without mourning, to care for while remaining carefree, to be involved *with* suffering without being involved *in* suffering. Knowing The Moment is perfect, recognizing your own inseparability from all that you survey, you are free at last to love the world, just as you are free to love yourself.

*You keep putting "God" in quotation marks.*
*Are you saying there is no God? And if so, that*
*there's no use in praying?*

There is definitely a God. It's you. You and everything around you.

But that said, in using quotation marks I'm saying that there is no "God" in the traditional sense of a king lording it imperiously over his creation, a judgmental boss on a heavenly throne that watches your every move and condemns you or promotes you according to your deeds.

But *that* said…I will tell you this: The Divine speaks to me all the time. Not in a deep booming voice, or any human voice at all…but when I ask a question of The Divine, I receive direct and speedy answers (often revealing a stunning sense of humor, I might add) in the form of synchronicities. I will ask a question, and the next song on the radio…or series of songs…will address that question in a startlingly direct way. I will be sad, and read something on the web quite by accident that specifically addresses my sadness and comments on whatever specific situation inspired that sadness. I have asked questions then randomly generated web pages that revealed the answers as surely as any *I Ching* divination.

All of creation is consciousness, containing and conveying information. You have only to ask, and to listen. I know this to be a fact from my own direct and repeated experiences. At this point in my life, these direct messages from The Divine are daily occurrences. Answers to my questions, or comments on my situation even when I don't directly pose any questions, are revealed through signs on the road, snippets of conversation, images in magazines, advertisements on billboards. Even personalized license plates have communicated meaningful things to me directly from "God"...or rather, the consciousness that animates The Moment.

The Moment is entirely formed from intelligence itself, which means every observable phenomenon contains information. The vast majority of this information remains opaque to our level of perception, but there's always more than enough information at your fingertips if you look for it. Once you widen your perception to receive these synchronicities, knowing them as direct communications from one section of your consciousness (The Moment) to another ("you"), you'll be stunned to learn that these messages are being sent constantly. You can access these universal insights on demand. Once this watchfulness has been fully integrated into your awareness, you'll receive synchronicities spontaneously throughout your day.

I do not know the exact nature of these replies. It would seem to me (though I only hypothesize) that not all of the divine consciousness constituting The Moment is deluded by the illusion of separateness that confuses most of us. In the *Bhagavad Gita*, Krishna, speaking in his role as an avatar of The Divine Ground of Existence, tells us "I support the entire cosmos with only a fragment of my being". In other words, The Divine has not invested all of itself in The Moment; there is a portion of that consciousness that remains outside, or above, this dualistic manifestation. I believe it may be that higher layer of awareness that responds to my questions, and can respond to your prayers.

Regardless of how it is manifested, that part of The Divine communicating directly with you will always address you in terms you will understand, in ways that are idiosyncratically specific to you, in your language, using whatever images, memories, and eccentricities that are meaningful to you. You may trust, and must trust if you're going to truly open yourself to this communication, that even the most incredible coincidences are the voice of The Divine. The Divine knows you intimately because it *is* you.

For example, if you ask whether or not you have a future with your current romantic partner, and immediately a song about heartbreak comes on the radio, say *The Breakup Song* by J. Giles Band, that's not a coincidence. It may have an even deeper level of meaning for you...perhaps the last time you heard it was at your senior prom, just before you got dumped. When that happens, you may rest assured it's an answer direct from "God" and not mere coincidence. It's a sign that your relationship is headed for the rocks...but then again, when the next song you hear is *I Will Survive*, it doesn't just mean your radio is stuck on an 80's station: that's the universal consciousness communicating you'll come out of this breakup just fine, and it'll be a positive development in your life.

I can tell you from experience, this consciousness is the most loving, kind, accepting, humorous and joyful presence I have ever felt. As a follow up to this book, I'm hoping to share my actual experiences with speaking to The Divine, culled from my years of extensive diary entries before these communications became too many to document. But this much I can tell you: The Divine is unspeakably compassionate, and it is waiting, patiently, always, for you to stop chattering in your own head long enough to hear its subtle voice.

Regardless of whether or not The Divine is also manifesting itself in The Moment as a presence not bound by The Moment, it is still nothing more than you yourself. In the process of manifesting itself as you, it sacrifices that larger perspective of itself as part of "playing the game". The very point of manifesting itself as you is to play the role of a separate being among strangers. Separation is the grand illusion...but you're always free to see through it if you choose.

*How can The Moment be perfect with so much extreme suffering in the world?*

There's nothing I can say to one who has experienced extreme suffering that can take that suffering away. As one who has endured deep loneliness and a profound sense of alienation all my life, I understand how insulting well-intentioned platitudes can seem coming from anyone who hasn't experienced the depths of your misery. I know it may seem insane to a person who has been raped, or tortured, or abused by a loved one, to hear that everything is not only okay, but perfect. At the worst moments of my depression, I could never entertain such an idea, for how could it possibly be right that I feel so worthless and alone? In the midst of suffering, the genius of the design of this grand illusion is that even one possessed of deep knowledge of The Moment will still experience extreme suffering *as* suffering, not as an experience observed from a safe place of emotional remove. Even Christ, enlightened as he was, cried out during the extreme agony of crucifixion: "My God, my God, why hast thou forsaken me?" [Psalm 22 KJV]. Extreme suffering is so powerful that even those of us fully awake to The Moment, observing such suffering from afar, cannot help but be moved by it.

I would like to communicate directly with those who even now find themselves burdened with some kind of terrible pain, so allow me to address you, the reader, for a moment as if this person were you. Were you to confront me with this question, coming from a place of deep pain, I would wish to make clear that I respect your suffering, and nothing I say in reply is intended to dismiss or minimize your experience. When I speak of the truth of The Moment in reply, I'm painfully aware that the message may seem, to one in the midst of great misery, disrespectful and possibly even cavalier. It is my hope, however, that the perspective I have to offer may ease your suffering to some extent, even in extreme cases. So please bear with me a moment as I proceed.

What can I say about extremes of human experience? I can tell you that extreme suffering can be an opportunity for sudden enlightenment. It isn't, for the most part, a trade that people would sign up for or consider equitable, but it is nevertheless true. In this book we've talked about how thought, mired as it is in language, is a barrier to direct experience of The Moment, and it is this direct experience that students of Zen and other Eastern disciplines seek. In the midst of great and overwhelming suffering, it is possible to bypass the chatter of thoughts and experience suffering as pure unfiltered being in The Moment. Throughout history, aspirants to enlightenment have subjected themselves to physical and spiritual torments, all in pursuit of the pure experience of reality known as enlightenment. Buddha himself, on his path to nirvana, deliberately subjected himself to years of extreme physical suffering as a forest-dwelling beggar. He eventually gave up on this path, achieving his final enlightenment using other methods, but undeniably this experience of suffering was part of the experience that led him to find nirvana beneath the Bodhi tree. (And to be perfectly clear, I do not advocate this approach in any way. I urge everyone against self-harm in every instance.)

On the other end of the scale, pure bliss can also be a direct path to enlightenment. Many a mystic has awakened to the truth of The Moment after receiving divine grace in the form of a vision or an epiphany...but there's no need for us to dwell on this experience, since nobody ever complains about bliss. It is noteworthy that, in addition to leading to enlightenment, terrible suffering can be a potent trap, anchoring us firmly in the delusion of The Moment by filling us with a greater sense of isolation, despair, and especially injustice. These negative feelings can grow exponentially under the influence of suffering when we deal with suffering not viscerally, as an experience to be lived, but intellectually as a problem to be solved, or as an injustice to be fought against, resisted, and resented.

The roots of suffering lie not only in the painful event itself, but also in the aggrieved sense of outrage you feel at the injustice of your suffering (Why is this happening to me?), the feeling of isolation that goes with suffering (I am solely experiencing this misery surrounded by those more fortunate who could never understand it), the desire of the suffering to end (for the agony is compounded by thoughts and hopes that it *will* end, keeping us from living in The Moment and forcing us to live in a hypothetical future), and the frustration over being powerless to bring about that imagined end.

For anyone who is experiencing, or has experienced, deep pain or horrific circumstances in their lives, I would never wish to show anything but respect and compassion for the reality of your pain; in discussing this question, I hope to offer you not a "cure" for your suffering, but a perspective that may alleviate some of your pain, and provide you with some cognitive tools to bring healing.

I would say first what I have said before — though the part of you that sees yourself as a separate victim of external circumstances beyond your control may find this offensive, even laughable, your suffering is as much in accord with your perfection as your joy could ever be. Know that the sacrifice of your suffering not only makes joy possible, it is your suffering that makes all the universe possible. One of the great magnifiers of suffering is the sense of its pointlessness; you are in deep misery, and you feel alone with a sense of terrible futility and helplessness. This is understandable, but not true.

Your suffering is essential to the very existence of The Moment itself. You are The Moment, and beyond it, The Divine. The Divine did not trap itself in The Moment by accident. It was not a clumsy oaf that slipped on some cosmic banana peel, banged its head, and slipped into a nightmarish coma of deluded manifestation. No — the consciousness that is you knew that, in manifesting a dualistic reality of seemingly separate forms, every attribute would require, and be defined by, an opposite extreme. To experience anything at all in such a universe, it knew it would have to experience suffering as well as joy, and it chose to do so willingly just the same, because the joy of manifestation was worth the suffering. There would be no way for this being to create a universe of only positive experiences, for how would anyone ever appreciate them without knowing negative experiences? Without cold rainy days, endless summer days would very rapidly lose their charm, would in fact slip entirely beneath the threshold of attention. We do not notice things in our world that stay the same. A knickknack that sits on a shelf for twenty years is a knickknack we cease to pay any attention to, no matter how fabulous it is. We would not only lose awareness of an endless summer day, we would actually cease to have any appreciation of any kind for it. It would simply be The World As It Is, accepted without a thought.

The Moment is the manifestation of change and motion — without different extremes of hot and cold, dark and light, here and there, this and that, how can there be change or motion? In a world of endless summer days, without death or illness, unchanging forever, where is there to go? What is there to change? What motion can occur? If food is always plentiful, there's no need to move around looking for it. Hunger would not exist. Neither would seasons exist, nor night, nor pain. One would never fear the roar of a beast in the dark jungle, but neither would one ever glimpse the moon on the water, the stars in their mysterious sky, or the unspeakable glory of a sunset. The less change there was in the universe, the more it would resemble the changeless realm beyond time that is our natural home, and so what would be the point of it all? Why bother creating a Moment of perpetual bliss when we already inhabit such a changeless and untroubled realm?

And so, when you are greatly suffering, the first thing that you can dispense with is the added suffering that goes with a sense of futility and helplessness. Allow yourself what comfort you may derive from the knowledge that your suffering supports the entire universe — not theoretically, not intellectually, not symbolically, but *literally* — your suffering makes The Moment possible, and in your suffering you are serving your purpose perfectly.

That's not to say that you were born to suffer, that it's your lot in life, that you deserve it, or that it is proper and shouldn't end. I am merely saying that you are The Moment, and at all times The Moment, being nondual, is both joyous and despairing, happy and sad, rich and poor, good and evil, and without that being so, it would cease to exist. And so, in your suffering, you are not unlike Christ. His suffering, his cross, is a powerful metaphor for your own pain.

Consider — without getting into the truth or falsity of any particular religious tradition, let us take this story at face value: Christ was God, and yet he chose to suffer for the good of everyone. Christ's suffering was in accord with God's design.

I put it to you that your suffering serves no less a purpose. Your suffering is just as sacred, just as meaningful, just as indispensable to all. You suffer that the universe may live. Consider: as Christ's suffering was a voluntary sacrifice he offered up willingly, you entered into your sacrifice willingly as well when you chose manifestation, and for the same purpose, for like Christ you are God (though unlike Christ you have forgotten this fact). But whether you remember or have forgotten your true self, it makes no difference in terms of your suffering. Your suffering is a sacrifice for the whole of creation, and so it is sacred.

This is not to say you asked for this misery, or that you deserve it; nor is this meant as a blasphemy against the sacrifice of Christ, though sadly it may be taken that way by some. My only aim is to help those of you who are suffering to see your suffering in a new light, in the hope that this light may be a beacon for you to find, in the midst of your storm of suffering, a safer harbor for yourself, with smoother waters…a harbor where you may experience a lessening of your pain.

All this said, I must also point out that while suffering is indispensable to The Moment, the same must be said for joy and bliss. Though I'm focusing on the question of extreme suffering here, I don't mean to imply that suffering is any more vital or valid than happiness. Nothing could be farther from the truth. If the consciousness that created this moment were malicious in nature, if it were masochistic or sadistic, there would be far less beauty and much more ugliness in manifestation. As it is, the goodness and beauty in the world outweigh the evil and ugliness…but only just enough to keep the illusion going that life is a terrible risk, and evil might just win! Fundamentally, your divine nature is playful. The

Moment is a grand adventure for that which knows nothing but ultimate safety, a chaotic vacation from the uniform peace of The Divine. And so as we continue discussing misery, in this emphasis I'm not saying that sorrow is more significant than happiness, but simply that happiness cannot exist *without* sorrow. Your joy, your peace, your spontaneous delight — they are all equally the point of existence itself. Experience, all experience, is at the core of why we're here.

In terms of dealing with deep suffering, awareness of The Moment can shield you from the compounding of pain that comes from a sense of injustice. When our misery is seemingly inflicted upon us by another — if we are abused by a family member, harmed in a violent crime, oppressed by our government — the pain is compounded, and our delusion of being separate beings trapped in a lonely universe is deepened by our outrage and our desire for revenge.

It's easy to see revenge is an additional burden we saddle ourselves with once we examine how we respond differently to various forms of suffering. To understand this point, consider — if we lose everything we own due to a hurricane or tornado striking our home, we do not entertain thoughts of revenge against the storm. It is a misfortune whose suffering we must simply bear, as we cannot pursue revenge against a natural event, a so-called "act of

God". And yet, when an individual inflicts suffering upon us, we often entertain thoughts of settling the score, of inflicting suffering upon them in kind. But when we truly know The Moment, isn't it clear that the actions of this person are an "act of God" too?

Revenge is a perfect form of delusion, reinforcing the idea of separate me being victimized by separate them, and instilling within separate me the desire to pay separate them back.

This idea only compounds your suffering. Relieve yourself, please, of at least this portion of pain. Remember that not only are you not separate from that person inflicting suffering upon you, but even more to the point, neither of you is doing anything at all. Your seemingly separate actions are in reality the action of the entire indivisible Moment, and so while there may seem to be a malicious element to your suffering, no matter how vividly evil the author of your pain may appear, at root your suffering at his hands is the same as your suffering the misery inflicted by a storm. I point this out not to negate the real pain of your experience, but to illuminate the truth that there is only The Moment, only the one action that is the one actor. Malice is a delusion of separateness, perpetuated by those lost in that illusion. It is a perception that doesn't actually change the reality of the event. And so, in the act of suffering at the hands of another, do not additionally burden yourself with hatred and revenge. This will only remove you from the consolation of remembering Who You Really Are. You may have no choice in experiencing your suffering, but you can at least refuse to surrender your higher knowledge of yourself as The Moment.

In the midst of terrible suffering, you may not be able to feel that unity with all of creation within you, but by allowing yourself to retain that conceptual realization, holding firm to knowledge of yourself as The Moment, you may at least lessen your suffering by accepting it, not as evil, but as a natural event to be forborne, with the peace that comes from acceptance — not acceptance of the inevitability of your suffering (if the chance to escape it comes, then by all means take it), but by the forbearance, free of hate and anger, that you use when riding out a storm.

The essential core of suffering is woven into the fabric of The Moment. Without that thread, its tapestry would unravel. There is no avoiding it. We all suffer — some more, some less, though who can really calculate the comparative metrics of pain? We all have different capacities to tolerate suffering, and so what one person may experience as discomfort, another may suffer as agony. I have lived most of my life with the sense of being an outcast. I have often internalized that emotion James Joyce referred to as feeling "like an outcast from life's feast". I had no refuge even in my own skin, because I hated myself. This low level constant misery…does it compare to being raped by your father, or abducted and tortured? I wouldn't presume to say it would, but I also acknowledge that none of us can know the pain of another.

There is no way to eliminate suffering, but there is also no need to reinforce it with harmful self-inflicted wounds. Misery is like a wall, and the best way to move through it is to disassemble it as best you can, brick by brick. Disassemble the pain of injustice from your wall — there is no injustice, only the random nature of the storm. Disassemble the desire for revenge from your wall — the seeming evil inflicting itself upon you is lost in delusion, and hating it simply isolates you from the higher awareness that is your greatest inner strength. Forbear your suffering without placing the responsibility for fighting it on your own head. As a victim of rape can make the rape so much worse by blaming herself (or himself) for "letting it happen", we never blame ourselves for not resisting a hurricane. All misfortunes are storms in the weather of The Moment. See them not as affronts, but sorrows, and try, if you can, to see all sorrows as temporary illusions that you, a timeless eternal consciousness, tolerate as the cost of manifesting all of creation.

Though you may feel horribly tainted inside from your painful experiences — abused, damaged, even ruined — know the true core of yourself is beyond the reach of any stain from anything that happens in The Moment. Nothing you do, and nothing done to you, can ever mar your beauty and perfection in the slightest. Though you have forgotten yourself by design, whatever you are feeling right now, in the end you will be, and secretly are even now, delighted that you took the ride we call existence.

Consider what a privilege it is, what a miracle, to be able to feel anything at all. Though we're used to our lives, and may even consider them ordinary or humdrum, they are anything but. What a glorious thing it is, to feel a breeze in your hair, the sun on your skin! How astonishing is it, to feel love, and how astonishing too is it to feel the loss that is heartbreak. None of these things are ultimately real, and yet this spell we have cast is so utterly convincing, so deep and so mysterious, that even the magician is lost in amazement at his own enchantment!

To feel anything is wondrous. Because we feel continuously throughout our lives, we tend to take it for granted...but consider this. Without manifestation there is only the peace of changeless certitude, without sensation, free of pain and woe. As beings with ample supplies of pain and woe, the prospect of peaceful non-manifestation can seem delightful...but shouldn't we acknowledge how delightful the opposite would be for a being free of sensation to feel anything at all?

Revel in The Moment, in every part of it. Strive to be aware of the miraculous game of existence while you're manifested. And for those times when suffering overwhelms you and you can think of nothing else, I bow to your suffering with gratitude, reverence, sorrow, and awe. Without your sacrifice, indispensable and sanctified, this universe would not exist. Without the possibility of great suffering, all experience would be as nothing. When you suffer, though you can't feel it, you are also all the joy in the world.

*Is there, then, no escape from suffering
in The Moment?*

The Buddha famously taught that the cause of all suffering is desire — in particular, the futile and doomed desire to permanently cling to impermanent things. All things must pass, for change is a constant in The Moment, and so attempting to hold on to things in perpetual motion leads inevitably to frustration and suffering. Even in the midst of the most perfect day imaginable, you can transform that day into a torment by focusing on the thought that soon the perfect day must end.

Our desire to stop the process of change when it suits us, to suspend The Moment once it hits a pleasant phase favorable to our comfort, is an impossible desire that leads to suffering. In the midst of a fabulous meal, you hesitate to finish it because you want it to last...but then what happens? As you linger over the meal, the food gets colder and colder the longer you hesitate, eventually losing most of its charm...and still the meal ends. Likewise, an anniversary can transform from joy into sadness if you love your spouse so much you can't bear the thought of another year together being gone. The awareness that one of you will surely die someday may intrude on the occasion...but what is this thought at root? It is the desire to cling to your love that transforms a celebration into a wake, happiness into mourning, just as the final three days of your Hawaiian vacation can become a misery when you spend your time lamenting the fact that you will return to work on Monday.

Now what do all of those scenarios have in common? In every single instance, the suffering results from imagining the future rather than living in the present! The Sage lives entirely in the moment, aware that he *is* The Moment, and so his suffering is greatly lessened. He accepts what comes as what is — when it is suffering he suffers, when it is happiness he enjoys it. So when you ask "is there no escaping suffering", the answer (as usual) is yes and no. If you recognize your inseparability from The Moment as the Sage does, you will escape suffering when you're not suffering. It's that simple, but for the vast majority of humanity suffering remains a constant misery. So much of our suffering is self-inflicted, continual fantasies about future unhappiness that intrude on present life. Clinging to the desire for permanence in an impermanent world inevitably leads to suffering, but even without clinging we have seen that The Moment cannot exist without suffering…at least not in its current form.

The Hindus hold that the time frame for manifestation is divided into four Yugas, or ages.

These ages are named after throws in a game of dice in descending order of excellence: Satya, Treta, Dvapara, and Kali. Satya, being the best possible throw, is the longest of the Yugas and the most perfect, a time of idealized, untroubled manifestation that lasts for 1,728,000 years...a golden age, in other words. The Treta Yuga, lasting 1,296,000 years, is a silver age of manifestation, during which some difficulties intrude on the perfection of existence. The Dvapara Yuga, lasting 864,000 years, is a time when there is a balance between good and evil in manifestation, equal parts suffering and joy. In the final Kali Yuga, lasting a mere 432,000 years, the positive qualities of manifestation are reduced to a quarter of all experience, and manifestation is largely characterized by destruction and suffering. At the end of the Kali Yuga, the godhead in the form of the goddess Kali goes on a rampage of destruction, ending the universe and forcing Brahman (The Divine) to awaken from its dream, returning to its untroubled ordinary state of bliss for 4,320,000 years at which point it chooses to manifest again.

Regardless of whether you regard this myth as metaphor or literal truth, the idea of Yugas makes a lot of sense in terms of The Moment. After all, look at this from the point of view of the unmanifested Divine: if you were going to manifest yourself into a situation, what would you want that situation to be? Initially you'd want it to be perfectly wonderful...

you'd be happy to experience the miracle of manifestation without any complications or worries. This Yuga may represent the state of the cosmos as it was forming...without the drama of personal interactions, greed, betrayal, evil, or death, manifestation would be pretty fascinating. The Divine would enjoy the simple processes of the formation of the physical universe without judgment or comment. The Moment — manifested as time, space, gases, particles, energy, radiation, fire — would exist without pain (for none of these things have nervous systems), without fear, without death...in short, without the illusion of separateness; The Moment would simply *be*, and this could be what the Hindus refer to as the Satya Yuga.

So you, being The Divine, would dwell in a perfect state of anxiety-free manifestation for a very long time...but after that what would you do? You'd be a little bored with that level of existence, and so you'd desire a change. Perhaps you'd decide to take the plunge and dive into the delusion of duality and separation, thus manifesting as life, as separate seemingly-autonomous organisms with nervous systems, creatures that would interact with and feed upon each other. Perhaps this development is conceptually equivalent to the Treta Yuga, a time where some pain is introduced...but what of it? These creatures, being primitive and of limited intelligence, though scrabbling for survival and suffering injury and death, would dwell thoroughly in The Moment, lacking the intelligence to inflict suffering upon themselves by imagining future calamities. Manifestation would thus become a drama of survival, absent the fretting and self-inflicted misery associated with beings intelligent enough to imagine terrible futures even in the midst of the most perfect present.

But this, too, would lose its charm after awhile...and so you'd eventually take the next plunge, choosing to manifest higher animals and human beings. This level of complexity describes our existence now. Be it the Dvapara or Kali Yuga, we exist in a state of duality, tormenting ourselves with the desire to cling to pleasant nows even as we remove ourselves from pleasant nows by imagining all sorts of miserable laters. Thus we can see the value of the Yuga concept, how it traces the evolution of suffering in manifestation. But the thing to remember is *none of these Yugas is in reality more perfect than any other!* Each Yuga reflects the will of The Divine as it plays at the game of manifestation. No Yuga is improper or tainted, regardless of the amount of suffering involved. All the myriad forms of existence are at root one perfect consciousness...so what is there to regret or to correct?

Suffering is not inescapable in The Moment. After all, we've all had happy days, haven't we? The Sage evenly escapes and falls into suffering as it comes, but never plunges him or herself into it by power of his clinging or his imagination. But in another sense, it is impossible to escape suffering entirely. What about simple physical miseries like injuries, illnesses, and starvation? Clinging has little to do with this level of suffering. To be sure, Buddhists would argue that when one is suffering a headache, it is the desire not to have a headache that compounds the pain. True…and yet just the same, my head hurts. Anyone who has ever suffered from a migraine would contest the notion that this particular misery would cease if only they weren't clinging. Christ on the cross primarily suffered from the immediacy of nails pounded into his flesh. His perfect enlightenment and unity with The Divine did little to mitigate that suffering; similarly, watching another suffering intensely, say in a hospital ward dying from a terminal illness, will inflict some level of suffering on even an enlightened individual who possesses empathy. This suffering may be leavened by enlightenment, the awareness that nothing exists that doesn't serve the purpose of The Divine, but true enlightenment is knowing The Moment as it is, as you are, and how can you know The Moment without realizing that suffering is as inextricable a part of The Moment as joy? What would joy even mean without the comparison of misery?

The Buddha was wise. Much of our suffering is self-inflicted, the result of trying to cling to pleasure while avoiding pain, the longing to find a happy place in the universe and then dwell in that spot exclusively all of our days...a desire which is clearly impossible. So if we accept the constant changing nature of The Moment, living in The Moment without judgment, without trying to cling to perishable things — meaning all things — we can remove ourselves from a great deal of suffering. We can enjoy the anniversary without needing a guarantee that our marriage will last another year, savor the meal while eating it without worrying about finishing too quickly, and revel in the last few days of vacation without fretting about going back to work on Monday.

But ultimately, true enlightenment lies in not clinging to the idea of not clinging. True enlightenment is accepting that a certain amount of suffering in The Moment is as perfect as its counterbalance, a certain amount of joy.

*Are you saying I shouldn't bother trying to make the world a better place? Since nothing is left undone, doesn't that mean I shouldn't worry about easing the suffering of those around me?*

No, it doesn't. There is no should or should not. A person manifesting compassion will be swept up by compassionate currents of action. A person manifesting selfishness will be swept up in selfish currents of action. Though innately I feel that working to alleviate suffering and save the Earth is superior to selfish action because of the way I manifest, I know it is not. There is nothing here in need of fixing, nothing that should be done, no way to act contrary to The Moment.

That said, if you feel motivated to act for the general good, your experience of life will be fuller. Remember the law of Karmic Gravity. When you are swept up in dark actions, your experience of The Moment will be dark. Act in accordance with the principles of kindness, generosity, and compassion, and your experience will tend to embody those characteristics.

Of course, we have no choice in how we have manifested...at least none in this life. But we always act in accord with our own natures. A good example of this is the story of the warrior Arjuna and his charioteer, Krishna. Preparing to lead his army into battle against an army led by members of his own family, Arjuna is overcome with grief. He can't bear to commit violence against members of his own royal family, even though they intend him harm, and so in the middle of the battlefield, poised between the two armies, he sits down, and tells Krishna he will not fight.

Krishna, being a direct avatar of God, tells Arjuna to snap out of it, rise up, and kill those bastards!

There and then, on the field of Kurukshetra, Krishna confides to Arjuna all the secrets of the universe. He tells Arjuna to be at peace...no one here is going to die in this battle. No one here will ever die! There has never been a time when this did not exist, nor will that day ever come. All this, Krishna tells him, is simply the divine play of Brahman (The Divine), and since Arjuna is a warrior, he should behave like a warrior and wage war! After all, he reasons, if Arjuna refuses to fight then everyone will think he chickened out, and what shame could be worse for a warrior than dishonor? Krishna is not advocating violence here...he's saying that a warrior is war, a scholar is knowledge, a farmer is his crops, and being paralyzed into non-action by delusions of guilt, fear, and consequences is a foolish waste of manifestation.

In short, The Divine made this miraculous Moment to play in. Each of us plays this game in his own way, according to his inclinations, his gifts, and his fortunes...but regardless of how we play, play we should! For if we refuse to join in, what a waste of a perfectly good universe!

That said, there is nothing that needs to be done, and you are free to act, or not, as you like.

*Isn't it a contradiction to say The Divine is
The Moment, but exists separately from it?
Isn't that a division of the indivisible?*

Remember what I said of The Moment in *The Book of
Answers?*

Words only reflect it;
Thoughts are bound by it;
Opinions flail within it;
*Consistency cannot confine it;*
Measure breaks against it.

We cannot impose consistency on The Moment
because our perspective is too limited to comprehend
The Moment enough to measure it for consistency,
and our language is too mired in duality to express
anything definitive about it. How can we, manifested
in an illusion, comprehend the truth beyond the
illusion when our every thought is mired *in* that
illusion? We can't even utter a sentence without
tacitly reinforcing the notion of separate things, with
nouns, distinct from other nouns, performing verbs
that are separate from themselves. We can't even
think a purely truthful thought because we express
our thoughts in language. We can say what The
Moment is *like*, but we can't say what it *is*, because we
are The Moment and the Moment can't be the object
of its own understanding, in the same way that water

can't dampen itself, and lips can't kiss themselves.

Contradiction and conflict are woven into the fabric of The Moment to keep it perpetually active. If The Moment were perfectly rational, then all would quickly agree on the best course of action in every conflict and things would unfold much more smoothly. We are not here to have things run smoothly, or to achieve universal peace. The Moment thrives on conflict...and so there must be irrationality.

Each point of view sees itself as correct and valid, even if that point of view is deluded, stupid, or insane. By nature, any manifested consciousness is incapable of being objective regarding its own state. The madman doesn't know he's mad, and so conflict with sane people ensues. Just as it should, for consciousness doesn't manifest uniformly. Not everyone is equally rational, intelligent, or even sane. The Divine reserves the right, in playing the various facets of existence, to manifest across all levels of cognition, even to the point of insanity — not the garden variety of delusion we all experience when believing ourselves to be separate, but actual clinical madness. To add to the richness of this experience, the consciousness chooses to manifest at every level of awareness, from genius to idiot to madman to turtle to plant to rock (yes, all forms of matter contain some degree of consciousness...after all, how do certain elements know to selectively bond with other elements to form water, or gold? Even at the elemental level of manifestation, there is some degree of awareness of "self" and "other").

Just as light can behave as both a particle and a wave, contradictions exist to make sure we never get a complete and perfect grasp on reality. To do so would mean the end of reality's usefulness as a mysterious playground! It's perfectly fine for small pockets of The Moment to become self-aware, there's nothing wrong with that; enlightenment is a wonderful state to exist in. But given that we are already enlightened, being The Divine at root, it would defeat the purpose of The Moment if everyone awakened at once and saw through the illusion of separateness. That would be a waste of a perfectly good reality! The Divine, in such an instance, might enjoy manifesting in that perfect awareness for a time (as it may already...I have no idea how consciousness is manifested in the aforementioned stones after all), but eventually it would get tired of playing, kick the board as it were, and start another game!

Setting up a reality where any and all propositions can be considered simultaneously true and false according to the various viewpoints expressing them guarantees we will never have peace, or ever reach perfect agreement about anything. Making light behave as both particle and wave keeps the physicists at each others' throats. Debates about my God being able to beat up your God are always good for keeping things stirred up. Conflict and contradiction are the Watchers at the Gate, like the Angel of Death standing vigil at the entrance to the Garden of Eden, making sure that Adam and Eve, having been "kicked out" of paradise for buying into the duality of good and evil through unwise dietary choices, play the game properly and are barred from returning to the truth of their perfection prematurely, ruining the game "God" so carefully crafted for their amusement and delight by sneaking back into the Garden!

We are not here to have peace. That may seem a depressing thought, but consider how dull The Moment would be without conflict. Conflict goes with the delusion of separation. The struggle between viewpoints would quickly end if one viewpoint were obviously correct, and argument is woven into the very structure of language. As we've discussed, thing doing things to things is essentially the way we perceive and express existence. The game must never become too predictable, and it must not end prematurely by everyone realizing the rules are silly, there are no winners or losers, and there is nothing to win beyond playing the game.

I mentioned the Garden of Eden before. Ancient religious texts are filled with stories that, though absurd on the surface, are actually profound allegories at heart. The tale of Adam and Eve's expulsion from paradise is pure genius in this regard. Consider: Adam and Eve exist in unity with God and all of creation in the Garden of Eden only so long as they do not taste of the fruit of the Tree of the Knowledge of Good and Evil. Upon sampling the fruit, Adam and his mate are ejected from their state of unity with creation, and driven out into the larger world of conflict, pain, and death. The fruit represents duality in the most literal sense possible — knowledge of the difference between the primal states of Good and Evil. Once Adam and Eve accept this perception of duality, they are sundered from knowledge of their state of unity with God and creation. They cannot exist in perfect peace any longer...they will know hunger, and illness, and pain in childbirth, and ultimately death...and yet, in losing a garden, they gain the larger world (and I can't help but think how dull that garden would get after one thousand years, much less an eternity).

Is it so difficult to see that, in accepting the delusion of This and That, The Divine "cast itself" out of its blissful unmanifested unity (paradise) to experience the harshness of manifestation and all its woes (the world)? The greatest truths can often best be expressed via the simplest stories.

Similarly, the story of the Tower of Babel expresses very succinctly the role that conflict and contradiction play in maintaining The Moment. In this story, mankind is united in peace as one nation. This is not in accord with God's divine plan, but even worse, humanity is building a great tower that will reach even unto Heaven, allowing mankind to invade the divine realm and be one with God! To prevent this from happening, God curses mankind with various languages, dividing the Nation of Man into many nations that can no longer communicate with each other, each tribe magically converted into speaking its own tongue. That's why to this day someone speaking unintelligible gibberish is said to be "babbling". This divine curse of separate languages derails the great construction effort, and starts up enough wars to keep mankind busy for the next several thousand years at least...and certainly too busy to try to reach Heaven again.

This story is yet another fascinating allegory for The Moment. "God" (The Divine) has actively manifested a dualistic reality, accepting for itself the roles of every creature and every division within that reality. While contained in The Moment, the various false identities adopted by The Divine (in this case, humans) are not meant to reject the idea of themselves as separate beings. They are not meant to work together to realize their underlying essential unity, thus regaining Heaven...what is the point of that? To prevent itself from remembering who it is and seeing through the brilliantly crafted illusion of

The Moment, The Divine has structured contradiction and conflict into the fabric of manifestation, just as in the story God divides mankind with various languages and conflicts. This guarantees the game will run a good long time, without the majority of creation seeing through the illusion upon which The Moment is built.

Consistency, it is said, is the hobgoblin of small minds. Aside from the practical utility of contradiction in perpetuating exciting conflicts and preventing premature enlightenment from disrupting The Moment, any consciousness powerful and creative enough to create a reality of this transcendent wonder and staggering brilliance is not going to let a few contradictions stand in the way of a good time.

Given the power of The Divine to create something of this breathtaking intricacy and genius, I don't doubt all sorts of atypical phenomena are possible within The Moment. Do I believe that if The Divine wanted to manifest a person who can levitate or walk through walls it would be thwarted by anything as inconvenient as gravity or particle physics? I can't say for certain…but I find it hard to imagine.

As a philosopher, it's difficult to avoid engaging in a little idle speculation from time to time, so forgive me if I indulge myself for a moment. Sometimes I wonder if we, possessing a latent power of creation (given our unity with the creative consciousness animating the universe), can occasionally create odd manifestations of anomalous phenomena without even realizing it. Could paranormal activity and manifestations (the Loch Ness monster, UFOs, telekinesis) appear in highly-localized instances when we unconsciously and spontaneously tap into the creative power of The Divine? These things might not "exist" for long, observed only by one person or a small group. Manifesting for a brief period in isolated instances, these anomalies might be subsequently unverifiable, existing only long enough to be seen.

We are all The Divine, whether deluded by The Moment or not. Is it unthinkable that some of us, spontaneously and even unaware that we're doing so, may manifest things out of thin air from time to time? Could certain yogis levitate? Exhibit inhuman endurance? Teleport themselves? "There are more things in heaven and earth than are dreamed of in your philosophy", as the Bard said. Mind, I'm not advocating this idea. There's no direct proof of it that I'm aware of, it's just me taking my imagination for a walk...but I provide this speculation solely as an example of how I try not to impose consistency and conceptual restraints on a process I know but do not understand. I know what it is, but have no idea regarding its capabilities. Nor would any of this make any difference regarding The Divine or The Moment, which is impervious to our ideas and labels.

*You say God does not judge us, there is no hell, and evil is basically an illusion. Are you saying that any religions advocating these ideas are mistaken?*

Religious doctrines and texts are expressed linguistically, and given that all language is structurally flawed, all religions start out handicapped by that restriction. Even this book, while expressing the truth of The Moment as best as it can, is struggling to communicate through the cumbersome burden of a language antithetical to its thesis! Still, at least you're reading this book in the language in which it was originally written. The mind boggles at how wildly an inherently flawed text will suffer further inaccuracies when translated from another language! If all language is flawed and imprecise, then any attempt to communicate the highest truth of existence using language requires the most consistent and scrupulous usage, coupled with a clearly nondualistic intent. Ancient religious texts, translated across many languages and edited by authorities using them to establish churches and power bases, are going to have serious problems communicating any ultimate truths accurately, even with the best of intents.

That said, there are certain old concepts about "God" that are flatly wrong. The idea that any omnipotent and omnipresent god would behave with all the tyrannical pettiness of an ancient Sumerian sovereign is preposterous. The authors of various religious texts tended to conceive of God as the creator of the universe, and therefore its king; naturally when trying to conceive of a King of all Creation, the ancient authors of various texts looked to the kings they knew as models of what that Ultimate King would be like. Kings of the ancient world were generally brutal, authoritarian, powerful and wrathful entities to be feared…so how much more so would be the King of Kings?

The problem with that idea is this: even in the most primitive religions, God is depicted as all-powerful. It would therefore follow that God would possess no fear. Where there is no fear, there can be no anger, because anger is a natural response to fear, a response to a threat of some kind. The idea that God could be angered by anything we mere humans do is ridiculous. The idea that a god sensitive and capable enough to create something as delicate and lovely as a rainbow could simultaneously be as primitive and quick to anger as a Mesopotamian despot circa 2000 B.C. is merely a poverty of imagination. (And, I would think, a far worse example of taking the Lord's name in vain than saying "god damn", for wouldn't taking the Lord's name in vain more precisely mean slandering the Lord by smearing him with our own base human frailties?)

AUSTIN DE LA PENA

Philosophies of the East like Vedanta and Taoism do not fall into this trap. They acknowledge the nondual nature of existence, but can be fairly difficult to grasp because they often try to get around the imprecise nature of language by expressing their truths in opaque poetry and perplexing koans. And as with all religions, since its founding Hinduism has been complicated with layers of ritual, superstition, and thousands of gods, mythologies, and traditions that obscure its simple truth; similarly, Buddhism has evolved into many versions to confuse matters, some more dogmatic than others, with subtle nuances that followers latch onto with stubborn fervor, convinced their shade of Buddhism is the one true Buddhism.

But in all religions, however flawed, there are gems of truth that survive translation, editing, and power grabs by religious authorities. It is interesting to note that the only gospels accepted as canon in the early Catholic church were those testaments that reinforced the status of The Catholic Church as the sole intermediary between God and man. Even so, the wisdom of Christ still shines through translation and selective editing in pearls like:

Judge not, that ye be not judged. — Matthew 7:1

Take therefore no thought for the morrow: for the morrow shall take thought for the things of itself. — Luke 12:34

Verily I say unto you, inasmuch as ye have done it unto one of the least of these my brethren, ye have done it unto me. - Luke 19:40

All these quotes indicate an acute awareness of the nondual nature of the universe fully in keeping with the truth of The Moment.

So to answer that question, religions are at best distorted reflections of the higher reality they reference in the flawed conventions of dualistic language. But some truths survive translation in all religions.

*Is there any sentence in the English language that can express The Moment without suffering from the dualistic flaws you describe?*

The idea that nouns are separate from verbs is a linguistic conceit, not a feature of reality. Everything you say in English (and other similarly-structured languages) is reinforcing duality, except perhaps for the sentence "I am".

In this case, "I" could be taken to mean The Divine, complete with the indivisible manifestation of The Divine that is The Moment, and therefore the sentence could be read as a declaration of existence. This expression is somewhat redundant, for if there is an "I" to proclaim in the first place, then it must obviously "am" (exist) as well. So while still burdened with the noun/verb construction of English, it is still expressing a truth about The Divine manifestation of The Moment. It would seem that the Burning Bush was onto something when it told Moses: "I am that I am"…as was Popeye, who famously said "I yam what I yam".

*Isn't it blasphemous, claiming to be divine?*

Many religious traditions recognize that man is imbued by his creator with a spark of divinity. Christ himself famously said "The kingdom of God is within you", and of course the Eastern religions make no bones about this. Some people may frown upon this view, but there isn't a view in existence that isn't frowned upon by someone. Still, to deter as many needless frowns as possible, I'll clarify what I'm really saying.

I know that between me and The Divine there is no division. Though some might call this heresy or blasphemy, I do not fancy myself as some supernatural all-powerful being of elevated status. I claim authority over no other, for there are no others to assert divine authority upon. I am as holy, as sacred, and as exalted as anything else that exists...but that's not as grand as it sounds, because the same thing can be said about *you*...you, and everyone else you know.

No one is above me or beneath me, better or worse. This knowledge is humbling, not imperious; joyful, not preening; liberating, not conquering.

I am The Divine.  And my hope is that, by the end of this book, you will realize that *you are as well.*

*Would an awareness of The Moment protect me from fear?*

The extent to which this knowledge can shield you from fear depends on how deeply you internalize it. As my awareness of The Moment deepens, I find myself immersed in a wonder that tends to overwhelm fear. That said, our bodies will always revert to reflexes of fear in response to direct threats no matter what we know because we're hardwired by nature for survival. You may well be a guru levitating in a diaper peacefully contemplating lotus blossoms, but when you see an eighteen-wheeler about to run you over you're going to be alarmed in most cases, regardless of what you know (though to be fair, the aforementioned levitator might well be like Neo in *The Matrix*, so completely realizing the whole thing is an illusion that he's not disturbed in the slightest by the idea of being flattened by a truck on even a reflexive level, but that sort of total remove is rare, and all I can say is that I can't levitate, I don't wear a diaper, and when I get cut off by some idiot on the road I cuss up a storm, the number of times I pound the steering wheel being directly relational to how close that car came to hitting me).

The thing of it is, I'm no longer perturbed at myself for getting perturbed, for getting perturbed is perfectly part of The Moment. Remember...you are perfect exactly as you are. You can toss this book away, go on living exactly as you have and never give these words another thought, and you'll be just as perfect as the Buddha ever was. In fact, you are the Buddha. You've simply forgotten it. And that forgetting is as much the genius of The Moment as the remembering of who you truly are.

*I understand the logic of your argument, but is there actually any scientific proof for what you're saying?*

Actually, there is. According to Quantum Field Theory, all particles are actually condensations of waves in fields that permeate the universe. We all grew up with the standard orbital model of atoms, electrons circling a tiny nucleus in discrete and isolated packets of matter existing as self-contained units. This idea was mistaken; it is now theorized that every particle in the universe is in actuality not a separate discrete entity like a pellet, but a perturbation in a field that fills the entire universe like a fluid. This field is not of uniform density; it bunches up according to the rather complex laws of quantum mechanics, and these waves in the universal field produce those field extrusions we detect as particles.

This means that every particle is a connected part of the same field. There is one field for each type of particle, stretching throughout the universe. Particles are produced as excitations in their respective fields resulting from higher energy states at the points of the particle expressions. All electrons protrude from the universal electron field, all quarks protrude from the universal quark field, and every particle in my body is a wave in the same field that is producing your body. We are all connected in this way…to each other, to our planet, and to the entirety of creation in the same way that all waves at sea are simply protrusions of the larger ocean.

I must emphasize one point here: Quantum Field Theory is not stating that all particles of a kind *spring into existence* from their corresponding field; it is stating that all particles exist *in connection* with their field inseparably...in other words, all particles *are* their field. While they exist, they exist as excitations in the field — not as ejected products, but as currently attached protuberances, like spines on a porcupine (to use a crude analogy...there's no way we can visualize such a complex process). And so science tells us that we are all, as the mystics surmised thousands of years ago, one unfolding universal process, along with the Earth, the moon, the stars, and the so-called empty space that fills the universe.

I say so-called empty space, because scientists have now determined that empty space is anything but. Computer-generated models based on quantum equations have illustrated what scientists variously call "zero point fluctuation" or "quantum fluctuation" — the vibration of the universal fields even at their lowest energy state. Animated simulations depict the restless movement of zero point energy in a vacuum, surging and flowing in a dance of potential manifestation — absent sufficient energy to manifest particles, but still lying beneath the surface of the phenomenal world like the unconscious mind lurking beneath verbalized thoughts. It is hypothesized that, at this lowest level of energy, all the many fields merge into one undifferentiated field, existing at the baseline of reality, simply awaiting the energy to manifest the particles of creation that make up existence. According to the conventions I've established in this book, that lowest level of manifestation represented by the zero point field would be The Divine, and the higher fields of existence would be The Moment.

Thus we see that under the umbrella of time, even in the emptiest of spaces, there is an underlying universal field that remains in constant fluctuation. Once energy condenses in this field, it extends into component fields and manifests that energy into the physical universe as particles. In this way, all particles exist as perturbations in fields. Which begs a question I've yet to see addressed by physicists: what is it that keeps these transient effects organized to form consistent physical structures?

Think about it: a mountain is comprised of matter. A mountain is a stable physical formation, but how can this be when we know that all the particles in it are not detached particles that exist on their own, but excited protrusions of bunched-up energy in a unified field? Just in your body alone, there are approximately $1.5 \times 10^{28}$ electrons...a number so vast there's no label in English for it, other than, perhaps, "uncountable". When you consider the mind blowing number of field protrusions it takes to form your body alone, or a mountain, or a planet, or a universe, it begs the question: How would these energy transfers clump together to not only form unified coherent structures, but persist indefinitely? How does this highly fluid field form and then maintain our physical bodies, evolving structures that persist for a lifetime and beyond?

I would maintain that these fields manifest stable matter in the same way that a mind can hold a thought. The forms of the universe maintain coherence because The Moment is maintained by the force of The Divine — by consciousness itself.

*Is there any specific proof that consciousness is a universal force as you describe it?*

Yes there certainly is. In 1935, an Austrian physicist named Erwin Schrödinger devised a thought experiment to illustrate the implications of a bizarre quantum property known as superposition. In this hypothetical experiment, the experimenter places a cat into a sealed box alongside a radioactive isotope that has a 50% chance of being released by some mechanism and killing the cat. The box is opaque, preventing any observation of what's happening inside for the duration of the experiment — in this case, one hour. The central question posed by the experiment is simply this: when the experimenter opens the box, will the cat be alive or dead?

The obvious answer seems to be there's a 50% chance the cat will be alive, and a 50% chance the cat will be dead...but according to the principle of superposition, that answer is incorrect. In actual fact, the cat will be both alive *and* dead until the experimenter opens the box and observes the result! Only then will the cat's potential states collapse into one definitive state. The cat will be equally alive and dead until an observer forces the issue, at which time the cat's fate will be decided!

Quantum entities can exist in multiple states simultaneously. This property is known as superposition. Until a particle is measured or observed, it occupies all its potential states simultaneously, only resolving into one definitive state upon detection; indeed, the mathematics seem to indicate that *all* possible definitive states of quantum objects *do* resolve...*each in its own universe.* In other words, anything that can happen does happen...which leads us to the theory of parallel universes.

This theory holds that in every event, every possible outcome forces the creation of a parallel universe identical to its original universe, only differing in the outcome of that event. Using Schrodinger's example, the cat is both alive and dead until observed, at which point two universes are created, one where the cat is alive, one where it is dead. Both universes continue to exist in parallel.

Schrodinger formulated this experiment to illustrate subatomic effects on a macro scale, taking the idea of superposition to an extreme to make his point. The idea disturbed him so much that he backed away from the theory altogether, choosing to devote his time to studying biology on a comfortably macro scale. Schrodinger formulated this experiment as an analogy only — this odd property of matter is thought by many to apply solely to subatomic particles and not to larger conglomerations of matter. Superposition does not apply to objects at the cat level of existence...or does it? After all, on a universal scale of solar systems and galaxies, a cat is relatively as small as a particle; what if matter at a higher order of magnitude and mass is still subject to superposition, splitting off universes? Some physicists believe this to be the case: every event, on any scale, may well spawn parallel universes to accommodate all possible outcomes.

While it's possible that anything capable of happening does happen, in our particular universe we don't observe the various outcomes, and so it seems contrary to common sense that such branching outcomes occur. Even so, thanks to quantum theory, we can now glimpse this counter-intuitive possibility and consider its implications. Events only transition from theoretically potential states into manifested reality in conjunction with conscious observation. In a very real sense, consciousness creates reality. And every action on the macro level, at least theoretically, spawns a new universe.

Think about it...if you're out for a stroll one afternoon and come to a corner, in one parallel universe you turn right, in another you turn left, in yet another you turn around and walk away, and in yet another the teenager texting in the Volkswagen runs you over. But that's okay, since versions of you continue to exist in each of the other infinite number of universes you've spawned in your lifetime, none of them more or less real than any other. Every action you take, every choice you make, is spinning off parallel universes. Multiply this by all other people, all animals, all the waves on all the oceans, every game of chess, every flicker of every candle, and every change in a particle's state...all branching off parallel universes with each minute fluctuation!

There is no word, no sentence, no human thought adequate to express the mystery and wonder of existence. Perhaps at this point you can truly grasp why The Moment is incomprehensible. We can know its mind-blowing infinitude through the feeling of awe, but we can never understand it, never hold even a fraction of it in our minds.

Essentially, superposition reveals a central truth about existence — consciousness is not only a tangible force in the universe, it is the central force underlying existence itself. That existence is The Moment. That consciousness is The Divine. That consciousness is you.

Try to remember that the next time you feel small, or alone, or afraid. You are infinite grandeur — not a piece of it, but all of it, across all universes...you are the unspeakable perfection of The Moment, exactly as you are.

*But how can I ever truly know* myself
*as The Moment?*

All paths lead to The Moment. You simply have to find the path that works best for you.

Many traditions consider meditation the surest means of attaining enlightenment. Over the twenty-odd years I struggled to know The Moment, I didn't meditate rigorously. I had a good amount of success in stilling my thoughts, but I had nothing like a regular practice, and those times I did sit in contemplation I didn't do it in accord with any particular tradition or technique. Though the ability to quiet my thoughts was important, it wasn't the key to my knowledge of The Moment; rather, it was my constant study, reflection, and theorizing that finally resulted in the writing of this book, which somehow shifted something inside me and led me to this knowledge, realized not simply in my mind, but throughout my being.

Once I knew The Moment for what it was, and myself for what I am, my (many) neuroses dimmed, my (often irrational) fears receded, my sense of self-loathing vanished, my past regrets became abstractions...all limits that had previously defined me were replaced with a constant awareness of and wonder at all I see, all I hear, and everything I encounter. This state of being in tune with The Moment, even when not fully realized as enlightenment, can be a valuable technique for those seeking this realization.

Absent the accident of "divine grace" or twenty years of reading everything about mysticism, religion, philosophy, and quantum field theory you can get your hands on, you can know yourself as The Moment by practicing constant awareness — making the conscious effort to be completely present in your life at all times, fully immersed in your surroundings as they are, without judgment of any kind.

When practicing constant awareness, you are fully present in the world around you, fully inhabiting it with all your senses open to your surroundings *but without the interference of thought.*

Want to try it? Go outside. Feel things without labeling them. Don't think "what a lovely day" or "it's really stormy"…see the sky, feel the sun, smell the trees, hear the rain. Truly experience the world as it is, without imposing concepts and words upon it. If a thought springs into your head — about an upcoming appointment, a grievance, a work assignment — just label it a thought, and let it pass from your mind without judgment.

That's the key: whatever you do, do it without judgment. And that includes *not judging yourself for judging!*

This is particularly important when you're attempting to meditate, because it's easy to feel like you're failing each time a thought intrudes! Here you are, sitting on the floor, trying to blank your mind, focusing on the point between your eyes, concentrating on your breathing, or chanting "Om" (depending on the meditation tradition you're following), and without warning the thought "I need to add milk to my grocery list" springs to mind. Damn! You thrust that thought away, resume your chanting, and then boom! You start thinking about filing your tax returns, or the new season of Twin Peaks, or taking your car in for its yearly inspection. As these thoughts intrude, you berate yourself for failing to keep your mind clear, separating yourself even farther from your awareness of The Moment with judgmental thoughts about your futile efforts. *Perfect, am I? That's a* laugh...*how can I be perfect if I can't even stop thinking for more than ten seconds? I'll* never *get the hang of this "Moment" thing! I feel like an idiot sitting here chanting! And I bet I even forget to add milk to my list when I'm done with this! I better do it now, dammit...* And so your session ends, and you can't help but wonder: what was the point of all that?

The point of meditation is not simply to still your thoughts; while that is certainly a component, the point of meditation is to realize *it has no point.* When you take up the practice of meditation in order to achieve something beyond meditation, you've already missed the mark. If you meditate because you want to be enlightened, this begs the question: what is this "you" that seeks enlightenment? The core consciousness that is your true self is already enlightened, so any part of you that yearns for enlightenment must be the deluded ego layer of your mind, that illusory overlay of memories and thoughts which believes itself to be separate from the rest of the world and in need of enlightenment! And so right there, your meditation practice is compromised, even before any thoughts intrude. Catch-22: the part of you that seeks enlightenment is precisely the part that keeps you from recognizing you're already enlightened!

That initial realization is the first benefit of meditation: there is nothing your individual ego can do to achieve enlightenment because your individual ego is precisely the barrier to enlightenment. It can take students many frustrating years of sitting around to reach this understanding...and some never reach it. It's a valuable lesson that can leave students flummoxed...if meditation won't do the trick, how can I become enlightened?

Firstly, I encourage you to meditate simply to meditate. Do not meditate with any particular goal in mind. Do not set up any rules or expectations around the experience. Find what works for you: focus your consciousness on that spot between your eyes, just above the bridge of your nose, center your awareness on your breathing, or chant something like "Om" slowly and rhythmically. When a thought occurs, do not focus on its meaning; simply label it "a thought", and allow it to move on without judgment or comment. Reduce that thought to a movement of The Moment, like the falling of a leaf, or the movement of a cloud, devoid of context or meaning. Eventually you may wish to consider: if I'm watching this thought move by, then what is the "I" that is watching? We tend to think of ourselves as our thoughts, identifying with the chatter that fills our heads during every waking moment, but when you meditate, when your mind is relatively still, and a thought pops into it, you can more easily question this state of affairs: from where did this thought come? Am I the thought, or the observer of the thought? This process can facilitate the attainment of enlightenment, but only if it is not burdened with the responsibility for delivering enlightenment. It's a fine distinction, but a very real one. Meditation, like life, is most valuable when it is pursued for no reason other than itself.

The same comments apply to the practice of constant awareness, which is simply a kind of reverse meditation. Instead of going within, you're going without, expanding your consciousness to the larger Moment. In many ways this can be more valuable than traditional meditation, but the same guidelines apply: focus on everything around you without mental comment, dismiss thoughts as they occur without judgment of the thoughts or of yourself, and practice constant awareness without any agenda beyond practicing constant awareness. This visceral realization of your total harmony with the larger world will shift your unfolding of The Moment in ways you can't imagine...but only if you don't approach it with expectations or demands.

Regarding enlightenment I can tell you this: as someone who knows The Moment, I also know that I am no more or less perfect than I was when I didn't know The Moment. Now that The Moment has unfolded me into enlightenment, I realize I was serving my purpose perfectly by being myself, by providing The Divine with the particular viewpoint only I could provide. At one moment I was allowing The Divine to experience its Austin-ness as a lost and ignorant fellow languishing in self-torment, and The Divine loved that game of pretend (after all, The Moment is entirely based on that game of pretend)! But that said, I am now allowing The Divine to experience its Austin-ness as a sage who knows himself to be The Moment, understanding that Sage Me is just as much fun for The Divine as Befuddled Me ever was!

And so, along with a direct knowledge of The Moment comes, perhaps even more importantly, a complete acceptance of yourself as you are, wherever you are. I am not "perfect" even though I know myself to be perfect…and that's perfectly fine with me. Though I still have times when I get afraid or angry, those moments are transient and stripped of any larger implications. At times when I curse and pound on my steering wheel because I'm stuck in traffic, I don't berate myself for forgetting the glorious bliss of The Moment and lapsing into petty rage; instead, I accept that the traffic and my frustration are the way The Moment is currently unfolding. I don't question it. I don't feel that I'm lacking or that I've failed. The Divine manifested The Moment precisely so it could get pissed and honk its horn in traffic. And it manifested The Moment so that, in yet another guise, it could look at itself over there, honking away and cursing, and laugh, saying "what an a-hole, acting like that". The Divine is traffic and open road, honking and quiet, self-loathing and self-loving, deluded and enlightened, all at the same time, constantly. It doesn't matter which of those states you're in at any moment, you're still The Moment, and you're still perfectly you, in any of your infinite shades, and once you truly know that, nothing can disturb you again, even when you're disturbed.

My advice is this: stop chasing enlightenment, and allow it to overtake you.

*But if chasing enlightenment only drives it away,
what can I do to finally know The Moment?*

Having read this book, you now know everything you
need to know. You know in your mind that you're
inseparable from The Moment. All you need to do
now is find a way to transfer this knowledge from
your mind to your heart, and then keep it there.

But how can you complete that migration from
thought to practice, from notion to realization?
Naturally you can never do anything without first
desiring to act. When it comes to finding
enlightenment, the trick is being *open* to it as opposed
to *requiring* it. Do not focus on becoming enlightened;
focus instead on becoming aware of The Moment.
Once you do so, enlightenment will eventually follow.
But if you approach gaining knowledge of The
Moment not for the sake of that knowledge, but with
a desperate lust for enlightenment, you will thwart
yourself, for the part of "you" that lusts is the part
whose very existence is contingent upon *not* knowing
The Moment. Your ego, that sense of yourself that
sees itself as separate from The Moment, the surface
chatter in your mind that identifies itself with your
memories and emotions, is not your true self. It can
never become enlightened because it is delusion itself!
As a result, you could think of your deluded ego as

your jailer. It entices you with enlightenment not because it thinks you'll become enlightened, but because it knows the more you chase enlightenment, the more enlightenment will elude you — a very good thing for your ego because it can only exist as a delusion of separateness in a dualistic universe!

And so, approach enlightenment as a prisoner planning a jail break. No savvy prisoner announces to his jailers that he is preparing to leave. He bides his time, and then slips away in the night, without warning. So too should you seek to escape the prison of your ego subtly, without alerting it to your intention. Never warn your ego that it's in danger of being obliterated by proclaiming "I'm going to become a sage now"! No...you're not trying to achieve enlightenment...you're simply meditating, practicing constant awareness, thinking about this book. You're just going out for a stroll around the neighborhood, not thinking about anything, opening your senses to the entirety of the day.

In this way, without alarming your ego, you stroll and you stroll, day after day, and before you know it, just like that...you've escaped your prison.

This is how it happened to me. I struggled for over twenty years to end my pain by attaining enlightenment. All these years researching and writing about the nature of existence, I hurled myself against dense walls of tightly packed concepts wedged into thousands of hefty pages, or slowly waded through extremely short and cryptic works, puzzling over mysteries couched succinctly in scraps of self-contradictory poetry. It was frustrating, discouraging, maddening... and I failed constantly. All because I didn't understand at the time the very thing you now understand: the "me" that sought enlightenment was the "me" that made it impossible.

This book proved to be my prison break. In writing it I wasn't trying to gain enlightenment...I was simply trying to write a good book. *This* was my meditation. *This* was my constant awareness. I stopped running...and so enlightenment found me.

In writing this, I had but one goal — to communicate my knowledge of The Moment to you plainly and simply, in a book that would be as short as possible. A great deal has been written about mysticism and quantum physics over the years, much of it dense and confusing. I wanted to take the opposite path...I wanted to write a book that someone could get through in one sitting, a book that would present the reader with both the mysterious poetry of existence expressed cryptically, as well as the secrets of existence expressed in plain language. I know that you, dear reader, are perfect as you are...yet I also know you wouldn't be reading this if you weren't still seeking The Moment. Very likely the question still remains foremost in your mind: What steps can you take to know The Moment?

In conclusion, allow me to summarize these useful techniques once more.

*Awareness is the key.* Train yourself to see the world *as* yourself. This is a form of meditation that doesn't involve sitting and chanting. It is a wakeful process that doesn't attempt to filter out awareness, but to embrace it totally, exactly as it is. It is like meditation in that you attempt to experience the world as it is without the interference of thought. Don't think "this is a beautiful day"...instead, try to feel the sun on your skin, sense the wind in your hair, hear the birds and the lawnmower droning lazily in the distance. Try to let the actual *experience* of the day fill the space that would normally be filled by thoughts *about* the day. Thoughts are linguistic symbols for a larger reality. Stop accepting the counterfeit currency of symbols and shift instead to the true wealth of actual experience.

In a way, this unfiltered awareness of existence is what is known as Zen. Countless volumes have been written about Zen, mostly to no avail because Zen, like The Moment, like The Divine, cannot be communicated through words. Instruction in Zen is generally conveyed through insolvable puzzles called koans (contradictory or nonsensical propositions designed to illustrate the futility of logical argument), years of sitting silently in prescribed postures trying to still your mind, and occasional sharp blows in the head from Enlightened Masters with bamboo sticks who are trying anything they can to snap you the hell out of your own head.

Aspiring Zen students are told that to master Zen and achieve enlightenment, students must abandon all desire...begging the question "how do I avoid desiring to stop desiring?" Zen is full of these conundrums, all designed to get you to stop thinking about enlightenment and simply recognize that you are already enlightened. You are already the Buddha, though you haven't recognized it yet, or you refuse to accept it.

The daily life of an Enlightened Master is pretty much identical to the life of an unenlightened student, the only difference being the Enlightened Master no longer clings to anything — not even his idea of himself, and especially not his idea of himself as lacking anything. He accepts himself, and the world, as he is, as it is. He is no longer troubled by things he's done wrong, or things he needs to do. To emulate his example and walk his path, train yourself to be very aware of your thoughts, especially negative thoughts. Don't judge yourself for having these negative thoughts when they arise, just be watchful in order to catch yourself in the process of having them.

Fretting over circumstances beyond your control, worrying about the future, judging yourself for your actions or other people for theirs, dwelling on past grudges...all these thoughts should trip your inner alarms, preventing you from being sucked into dark places long enough to realize: this is a negative thought.

At first this will seem futile to you. Even stopping yourself and recognizing the thought won't help you to stop fretting, stop judging, or stop feeling angry. But when you practice this discipline of awareness long enough, it starts to become a reflex. This is a valuable reaction to cultivate, because you must be able to recognize these negative thoughts before you can neutralize them and, eventually, correct them. Once you do, you can take that thought and say "no, this thought is an illusion because I know all action is The Moment, and I am united with all things". You can remind yourself of this when you're angry at yourself for screwing something up, for speaking harshly to a loved one, for being angry in the first place. You can remind yourself of this when you're feeling lost, or when someone mistreats you, or when you're afraid of dying...in moments of sadness, as well as in moments of joy.

Eventually, applying this awareness with consistency, you'll short circuit the ingrained thought processes that spawn these thoughts. Once that happens, you'll be able to start correcting them. This is how I broke myself of the habit of saying "I hate myself", by relentlessly stopping and correcting myself every single time. If you correct these thoughts long enough, you'll internalize and cultivate your larger awareness of The Moment — all action is The Moment, and you are united with all things. You'll reach the point where you're free to act, knowing it isn't you executing the action, but the whole of The Moment. This will happen more and more frequently, until finally you never have to stop yourself. You'll always recognize your actions as the unfolding of The Moment. And you will do less and less every day until finally you do nothing at all. And lo and behold, you'll find the universe keeps on unfolding without your ego's personal responsibility…and nothing will be left undone.

In this process, many aspiring Buddhists and students of Zen are at a disadvantage due to the reluctance of their traditions to engage in metaphysical thoughts of existence beyond daily life. Certainly Buddhism and Zen are wise practices that can lead their practitioners to awareness of The Moment, but without addressing the root nature of reality, without that understanding of themselves as existence itself, students seeking enlightenment struggle all the more with subduing their thoughts and desires for enlightenment. It can take such students a long time to realize that enlightenment is accepting their thoughts and desires as they accept the wind, and the rain, and the cry of a duck over a still lake. No one questions the rightness of the rain; you are equally beyond question, equally the play of The Moment.

You have a head start over these noble aspirants. You have read this book, and have a perspective many of them do not have when they're starting out. You know you don't have to struggle with who you are. All you have to do is accept your own condition as perfection, then accept everyone else in their perfection, and simply stay aware of the miracle presented by every moment of the day, which is The Moment. Which is you.

You can also come to know The Moment by fostering a sense of wonder. Try not to ever look at anything as ordinary. Keep in mind, while doing even the most mundane and boring tasks like washing dishes, the sheer wonder of the process. As water streams into the sink, reflect that those particles are not separate objects, but extrusions from a field...the very field that is currently extruding you. Think of all the possible paths available to each of those chaotic water particles, and how each possible path has just spawned another universe. Think of the light streaming in through the window, photons that left the sun nine minutes ago according to your perspective, though from the photons' point of view, traveling at the speed of light as they were, the trip was instantaneous due to relativity. In other words, truly allow this book to permeate your awareness, and make that awareness constant. Knowing what you know, how could you ever look at anything again without feeling the elation of wonder?

Be grateful, every moment you can, for the miracle of manifestation from potentiality. And more importantly, don't get down on yourself when you forget to be grateful; when you find yourself bored, or angry, or frustrated, don't hold this against yourself. Remember that you're perfect exactly as you are, even when you're bored and ungrateful. In a way, getting lost in the lovely illusion of The Moment is the highest compliment you can pay it. You're here to get lost, after all…that's the point! The Moment is supposed to beguile and obscure, to dazzle and befuddle…it is the greatest magic trick in existence performed by the greatest magician of all, a trick so magnificent the magician even fools himself with it!

Clear your mind of thoughts, and be fully present, always. Don't inflict suffering upon yourself by clinging to impermanent things, or by surrendering awareness of The Moment to thoughts of imagined futures. The present is the only slice of time that actually exists. Live in it entirely.

Know that nothing is required of you or expected of you. Know there is nothing to win, and nothing to lose. Or failing that, pretend you do until you believe it. You are perfectly safe, always. No one dies; nothing is ever lost except the delusion of separation.

All that said, you can play as you will. If you're happy believing yourself a separate mortal born into a strange world, subject to death and threats of eternal judgment by a God who acts like some kind of medieval despot, by all means do so — The Moment was, after all, made to give you that impression and you're playing the game hard. Those illusions, those flaws, are precisely the point...but that said, the Divine doesn't care how you play. If you want to peek behind the curtain and realize the truth of the matter, that the Great and Powerful Oz is not at all what he seemed, and Kansas was always just a heel-click away, Oz will not mind.

The Moment can be lived in any way you desire. But recognizing The Moment for what it is can free you to play a more joyous game, a less stressful game, a game that is the greatest ever conceived.

This book is your invitation from The Divine to relax secure in the truth that you are The Moment, and nothing you can do can mar its perfection. You can do nothing wrong. You can do nothing at all...and yet you do everything.

# ABOUT THE AUTHOR

Austin De La Pena is an enlightened philosopher dedicated to spreading awareness of The Moment.

A survivor of depression, Austin seeks to help others realize their innate perfection and feel harmony with all of creation. He can be contacted at:

austindelapena1@gmail.com